A DAY TO REMEMBER

"Although I see other dolphins every day and never tire of their friendly exuberance, I still remember Tuffy as a special individual. I have since seen dolphins that could dive deeper and swim faster, but none that showed me as much cleverness and apparent understanding of his human companions.

"I remember one day, one of many similar days, when the sun shone from a bright blue sky on a crystal clear Pacific. We spent that day at the dive buoy watching Tuffy dive into the smoky blue abyss. Then we waited expectantly for his dark eyes to appear out of the depths as he watched us watching him. I can see him riding large waves, I can see the crescent star as he leaped above the surf chasing anchovies, and I can hear his squeal of glee. As we motored in, Tuffy riding the stern wave of our boat, I remember thinking: for me, life can't get any better than this, and if I could translate his thoughts into human terms, I bet Tuffy might be thinking the same thing."

DR. SAM RIDGWAY

THE DOLPHIN DOCTOR

A pioneering veterinarian remembers the extraordinary dolphin that inspired his career

by Sam Ridgway

FAWCETT CREST • NEW YORK

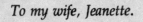

To my wife, Jeanette.

If the cleverest of all mammals is
man himself, the most excellent among
the others is surely the dolphin.

Anthony Alpers (1960)

Introduction

When I graduated in 1960 from Texas A&M University's College of Veterinary Medicine, I had no inkling of my imminent career in the study of marine mammals. I knew absolutely nothing about dolphins. Of necessity, my future work was to be one part adventure, many parts trial and error.

Except for a period from 1970 to 1972, during which I earned a Ph.D. in neurobiology from Cambridge University in England, I have worked full-time with dolphins from 1962 to 1987 under the employ of the U.S. Navy. I share with the relatively few other scientists who study these small whales an interest in the animal's adaptations to life in the sea—sonar, diving, swimming, and underwater communication—as well as the desire to protect and conserve the species.

But my personal experience with the study of dolphins differs: A single dolphin inspired my whole career. This book tells the story of my relationship with the unique bottlenosed dolphin called Tuffy, with whom

I worked closely from the time of his capture until his death eight years later. During this time Tuffy worked not only in the laboratory but also swimming freely in the open sea, returning to us when we called.

When Tuffy died, I grieved almost as much as if he had been a beloved family member. My book, then, could not be simply a report of a scientist's work or a naturalist's account of a species. On the contrary, this book is a personal record of my experiences, and it is an encomium—an unabashed story of praise—about one special dolphin whom I still regard as my friend from the sea.

The relationship began in 1962, when John F. Kennedy was president. The country was committed to putting men on the moon. As a young veterinary officer in the U.S. Air Force, I was infected with the enthusiasm of this era while working with a group of space scientists at Point Mugu, a navy missile base on the California coast. Even more exciting to me was the fact that the mysteries of the sea also attracted some of these scientists; they thought the exploration of the ocean was just as important as venturing into space, and they had begun plans to study dolphins. They wanted to know how dolphins could swim so fast and silently beneath the ocean's surface, how their sonar worked, how deep they could dive, and more. The answers to these questions might be useful to humans trying to live and work under the sea.

At the inception of dolphin research at the California missile base, there was another connection to space research: the potential for communication with extra-terrestrial beings. Dr. John Lilly, a physician and neurophysiologist, had just published a book, *Man and Dolphin,* in which he argued that scientists should learn to communicate with dolphins to prepare for communication with intelligent life in outer space. Knowing of the dolphin's large, highly convoluted brain, similar in size to the human brain, many scientists were taken with Lilly's ideas, and I was among them in the beginning.

Our small laboratory at Point Mugu was to become a focal point of dolphin research in the 1960s. Many scientists from major universities came there to study our dolphins. As the first veterinarian to work full-time with dolphins, I faced unique problems in my job of keeping these mammals healthy for the scientists. Little was known about dolphin medical care or physiology. We did not know how to anesthetize a dolphin for surgery or even how to take a blood sample for diagnostic tests, let alone how to interpret the test results.

Studies with Tuffy and other dolphins provided the information necessary to practice medical science with dolphins. But Tuffy was unique in several ways. He was the first truly domesticated dolphin, adapted to life in intimate association with humans. Despite his occasional displays of ill temper and pouting, Tuffy's reliability, adaptability, and sociability led us to insights about how warm-blooded mammals have adapted to life in the sea.

Once Tuffy began to work with us, swim beside our boats, dive with us, fetch and carry, and do useful tasks, we began to think about dolphins in a different way. We were dreamers in an optimistic time. We were about to invade the subsea world as ill-adapted strangers; talk of colonizing the sea abounded. What better way to get insight about surviving the hostile environment of the deep sea than to work with a mammal supremely adapted to living there?

The man-in-the-sea program gained urgency when, in April 1963, the U.S. submarine *Thresher* sank with 129 men aboard. The navy decided it urgently needed the capability to work in the deep ocean. A navy medical officer, Captain George Bond, took charge of a project called SeaLab, which aimed to make it possible for humans to live and work for long periods on the sea bottom, down to 800 or even 1,000 feet. During 1964, in the warm waters off Bermuda, navy divers lived for a week in a sea bottom habitat called SeaLab I. The following year Captain Bond and his coworkers took on a much more ambitious task when they placed a second, larger habitat at a depth of 205 feet about one-half mile off the shore of La Jolla, California. Three teams of ten divers, or "aquanauts," spent about ten days each on the ocean bottom.

At the time SeaLab II was judged a huge success. There was so much publicity that most of the aquanauts became famous, if only for a short time. My dolphin Tuffy, brought in as a member of the SeaLab team, came in for his share of renown. Captain Edward Beckman, a senior navy medical officer, told me that the work with Tuffy was the most important thing that came out of SeaLab. Of course, mine were willing ears for such information. At SeaLab II and during preparation for SeaLab III (which eventually was canceled due to the death of an aquanaut), Tuffy showed us that marine mammals could perform some of the tasks that had been envisioned for aquanauts. To this day sea mammals do these things reliably and economically. Diving at six hundred or a thousand feet in the ocean is a dangerous undertaking for humans, but for

Tuffy this was a natural act of daily life, almost entirely without danger.

I suspect that if we had not been lucky enough to meet Tuffy, our work would not have been nearly as successful. Extraordinary human beings such as Isaac Newton, William Shakespeare, and Albert Einstein have framed the progress of humankind. Among dolphins, Tuffy was such a giant.

I begin my story not at the outset of my relationship with dolphins or with Tuffy but on the very day in September 1965 when Tuffy and those of us who worked with him were put to a crucial trial: the completion of the final day's tests at SeaLab.

As our dinghy settled into the trough between two ocean waves, I momentarily lost sight of the navy's massive SeaLab support ship *Berkone*. Nearby, a dolphin arched into the air. A large crescent-shaped scar along his right side shone palely for an instant before he disappeared into the sea. My knuckles whitened on the gunnel, and as the dolphin failed to reappear, I could not refrain from pleading aloud, "Come on, Tuffy. Don't leave us now."

Unzipping the collar of his wet suit, Marty Conboy kneeled on the rocking dinghy's thwart to get a better view over the choppy sea. He slapped his knee in frustration and bellowed into the wind: "That porpoise! Where is he going?"

With an exaggerated sigh Marty sat down in the boat and leaned back as if exhausted. He glanced slyly at me, and I recognized the familiar twinkle in his eyes that meant he was about to give me a hard time. "Hey, Sam, why didn't you train some timing into that porpoise? We've got half the navy's ships, aircraft, and cranes out here, and all of them are sitting around waiting for the return of Tuffy, the bottlenosed dolphin. You're sure gonna catch hell if he keeps swimming toward Hawaii."

Wally Ross, my other companion in the dinghy, pulled a strobe light from the water, where its clicks and blinks had been signaling Tuffy to return to us. He turned and joined Marty in the ribbing. "Yeah, Doc. Why didn't you tell us this might happen?"

"I could ask you the same thing," I said with chagrin. "You guys are supposed to know all there is to know about dolphin training. At least that's what you've been telling me."

"Sure, we're awful good," Wally answered. "But there's one thing we never could do worth a darn, and that's teach Tuffy to work exactly on our schedule."

"That's the truth," Marty agreed. "Tuffy comes back when he damn well pleases. And I think he knows just how long to wait before we start to panic."

Wally and Marty pulled the dinghy close beside the landing craft that lay at anchor near the *Berkone*. From this vantage we could try to signal Tuffy again. As Wally put the strobe back into the ocean, we all peered helplessly across the blue Pacific, wishing for a glimpse of the gray dolphin.

But Tuffy stayed hidden. Back at San Diego, a helicopter was poised to take off as soon as the pilot received our go-ahead. Above us, on the high deck of the landing craft, seamen stood by with a crane to lift the dolphin on board. In our three years of work with Tuffy, this was his most important day yet, and here the three of us who felt the most responsible for his success sat in a dinghy, growing more nervous each minute. Swearing into the wind, Marty switched off the outboard engine and sat upright, gazing into the sea. Waves lifted our small boat and banged it against the landing craft's hull. Struggling to keep our balance, we held tightly to the wooden gunnel.

Suddenly, Marty yelled, "There he is by the *Berkone*." A hundred yards away, I saw the gray dorsal fin. The flukes came up, then disappeared as the dolphin dived.

Wally removed his dripping headgear, a straw hat in which he stowed his smokes. Retrieving a soggy, crushed pack of Camels hidden behind the sweatband, Wally drawled, "Well, fellas, it looks like he's about ready to work." He stroked several matches against the moist sandpaper of the packet; finally, the last match flamed. Wally cupped his hands expertly around the precious fire and soon was drawing smoke. The tobacco seemed to renew him. With fresh energy he pitched the strobe over the side once more and leaned out over the water to call Tuffy. "Come on porpoise, let's go home." His bright expression changed to one of disgust as sea spray quashed the fire in his cigarette.

I put our hydrophone in the water and listened through headphones. Although I could barely hear the click of the strobe from its location just a few feet underwater, I knew that Tuffy's keen ears could hear it well, even from a few hundred yards away. We waited. On the ocean bottom two hundred feet below our dinghy, a team of SeaLab II aquanauts worked near their quarters, a specially outfitted metal canister. During the past several days Tuffy had proved he could work with the divers, delivering mail and supplies and practicing rescue techniques. Perhaps he had decided to pay the divers one last visit.

After what seemed to us an interminable wait, the

dolphin suddenly bobbed into view again. Tuffy poked his head above a wave as if to say, "Oh, were you calling me?" Gliding just beneath the surface of a swell, he sped toward us.

"Get that sling into the water," Wally ordered. I grasped one end of the dolphin's hammocklike sling while Marty held the other end in the stern. Reaching as far out as possible, we draped the canvas sling in the water. Wally held the strobe near its forward end, and without hesitation Tuffy slid across the canvas and touched the strobe with his snout. He bowed his body to take a fish from Wally, then relaxed as we lifted the sling, encircling him with canvas, and held him against our boat. Every twenty or thirty seconds, Tuffy's blowhole softly popped as he exhaled. Although I had worked with Tuffy for three years, I still marveled at the dolphin's submissiveness in these circumstances. Wrapped in the canvas sling, pinned against our boat, and bombarded with engine noise, he lay serenely and waited.

"Headache!" yelled Marty, calling for the heavy steel hook from the landing-craft crane above us. Marty reached for it, attached the rope harness supporting Tuffy's sling, and gave a thumbs-up sign. A whirring above our heads began, and Tuffy in his sling swung high into the air.

Anxious to help the men bring our dolphin in safely, the three of us scrambled up the ladder attached to the gray steel hull of the landing craft. Seamen on deck pulled at the lines to control Tuffy's swinging hammock. Just as I reached the top step, I saw Tuffy begin a slow descent to a foam-rubber mattress spread out on the deck. Out of his element, Tuffy was motionless and helpless, completely dependent on our care. When

I parted the canvas to examine him, the dolphin opened his mouth in a mild threat he often showed me. I drew back. All things considered, I could see his aggressive spirit was intact.

As we prepared to transport Tuffy to the helicopter pad, seamen in blue dungarees clustered around to stare and ask questions. Divers in black wet suits hoisted tanks and checked their gear as they readied themselves to enter the sea. Meanwhile, Tuffy lay on his side, his large, dark brown eye alertly following the movements of the busy sailors and divers. "You crusty porpoise," Wally said. "Do you have any idea that you are the center of attention? I wish I knew what goes on inside your head."

Our helicopter lifted off with Tuffy aboard and headed north toward our research facility at Point Mugu, near Los Angeles. The *Berkone* and the landing craft with its cranes and gray machinery grew smaller and smaller as we rose into the sky above the vast Pacific.

Tuffy lay in wet canvas on a rubber pad, while Marty stroked the dolphin's flukes with a wet sponge. Wally smiled down on the dolphin he had trained. He shouted over the din of the helicopter engine, "Tuffy, you've done it, you've done it."

What Tuffy had done was to prove that a wild dolphin could be trained to work with humans in the scientific investigation of the sea. Trained and then released without a tether, Tuffy dove to the sea bottom to perform tasks difficult or impossible for humans. Marty and I also were jubilant. We were dazzled by this animal who seemed so willing to work for us, despite his occasional brief disappearances. We knew that Tuffy had functioned as more than a beast of burden and a pair of sensitive underwater eyes and ears. The dolphin had served as a potential lifesaver in a human-animal team.

Under different circumstances our triumphant return trip to Point Mugu no doubt would have been spent in happy conversation. But since the thunder of the helicopter's engine and rotor blades made it impossible to converse without shouting, I sat back and contemplated. Remembering the events that had brought me to this moment, I felt almost incredulous at my good luck.

My career as a dolphin doctor had begun three years earlier, in 1962, during my second year of duty as base veterinarian at Oxnard Air Force Base, near Camarillo, California. That fall my obligation for air force duty was due to end, and my wife, Jeanette, and I had been weighing future career options. The longer I worked in animal health care, the more I realized that my major interest lay in some area of research. Although I enjoyed the practical work of veterinary medicine, my curiosity led me to probe unanswered questions about animal physiology.

During this time I also worked with animals at Point Mugu, a nearby navy base, where I had met Commander Lee Hall, a scientist who specialized in aviation medicine. Dr. Hall had filled me in on a navy dolphin research project that was just getting underway. One day, when I was conducting a pet clinic at Oxnard, Dr. Hall telephoned me. He came to the point quickly. "Our last dolphin died this morning," he said.

"The last one?" I asked. "I thought you had three dolphins."

"Yes, they didn't last long. I had hoped to get you over to look at the dolphins before now, but the researchers here have been working with some medical doctor from USC. I guess they were worried about too many cooks . . . that sort of thing. Anyway, they now would like you to come over and do an autopsy on the dolphin that died today—if you can, that is," he added hastily.

"Well, I don't know anything about marine mammals except what I've read in a magazine article or two," I answered uncertainly. "But I'll be glad to give it a try."

As I assembled my instruments for the dolphin autopsy, I grew more and more excited about the prospect of learning something about a species new to me. I drove several miles from my veterinary clinic at Oxnard to a white sandy beach beside Mugu Lagoon. There my navy friends showed me a dead dolphin laid out on the sand in a long, gray wire basket.

Dr. Hall introduced me to two sailors named Bill Scronce and Marty Conboy, who had agreed to help me. "I've never seen a dolphin in the flesh before," I said. "I know it's a mammal, and I can see it has eyes and a mouth. Maybe we can start from that end."

"That sounds like a good plan," said Bill with a grin.

Opening the elongated lips of the dolphin's snout, I was startled to see numerous white teeth curved inward at the tip. Feeling deep inside the mouth, I found two thumb-size masses, one on either side of the throat. Enlarged tonsils, I thought. I also noticed that the gums were ulcerated. Beginning with these cursory observations, I set out to do the autopsy.

Bill had a pleasant, ruddy face. His bright eyes followed every move I made, and he chatted continuously as I laid out instruments on a makeshift table. Marty appeared much quieter, even taciturn, but as the three of us worked, I recognized his quick, subtle humor.

"They never told us what killed the first two," Bill told me, as he and Marty heaved the dolphin onto carpenter's sawhorses they had placed in the sand. I observed that the animal's back was almost black. Imprints from the wire basket in which it had lain marred the dull white underbelly.

"I'm not sure I'll be able to tell you either. But maybe we can learn something from this dolphin that will help us to save the next sick one," I said, looking hopefully toward the empty pool.

The two sailors helped me disassemble the dolphin, from the tip of its pink, scalloped tongue to its black, streamlined flukes. For me the dolphin autopsy was like a journey taken over strange hills and valleys. We put the dissected parts into bottles for later examination under the microscope, collected fluids for laboratory tests, and, finally, prepared to remove the brain for preservation and study.

As a veterinary student at Texas A&M University at the end of the 1950s, I had learned how to remove the brains of dead creatures of all sorts, from mice to mules, but never of cetaceans. Now as I carefully chipped away at the dolphin's skull to expose its brain, I was surprised by the thinness of the bone. Soon I saw that the brain was large and deeply convoluted. In my veterinary studies I had learned to associate these characteristics of brain anatomy with conceptual thought, the mental capacity that only humans were supposed to possess. It seemed clear to me that dolphins were something special.

"The brain shows no sign of disease, so far as I can tell," I said, as I plopped the parts into a jar of Formalin that Bill tilted toward me. I went on to examine the lungs and from their appearance concluded that the dolphin had died of pneumonia. Later examination of the preserved specimens confirmed my diagnosis.

A week after the dolphin autopsy Dr. Hall assembled some of the scientists and naval officers interested in the fledgling dolphin project to hear my full medical report. After I had spoken, Dr. Hall leaned back in his chair and puffed meditatively on his cigar. "The navy's had four dolphins, and they all died," he said, glancing down the long table at his associates. "If this project is going to get off the ground, we will need a full-time veterinarian. I think Dr. Ridgway here is the man."

I grew somewhat uncomfortable as the assemblage talked around me, discussing whether the project could afford to hire another person and whether the necessary approvals for a new position could be obtained. In the end the group agreed to let Dr. Hall study the problem.

"I'm not sure I can work it out," he said to me back in his office, "but I know you should keep studying about dolphins." Looking over his half-spectacles, he pointed at me with the chewed end of his cigar. "You ought to learn about their medical care, just in case we call on you to treat one."

"I'll certainly give it a try," I replied, "but I have never touched a live dolphin or even seen one up close."

"Well, I've got a solution for that. I've come to know Wally Ross, the dolphin trainer down at POP."

"POP?" I asked blankly.

"Sure, come on Tex! Where have you been? POP, Pacific Ocean Park, that big old amusement pier down in Santa Monica. Everybody in southern California knows POP."

A few days later I visited Wally Ross and his associate, Morris "Mo" Wintermantel, who ran the sea circus at Pacific Ocean Park. When I first met these two men, I did not guess how much they would teach me about dolphins. I did know that I had encountered some memorable individuals. Wally, a tall, slow-speaking Missourian, had run away from his family's farm to join the circus. During his years with the circus, I learned, Wally had become an animal trainer, working with dogs, elephants, chimps, and sea lions. Now, he told me, he concentrated on dolphins. "I've trained just about all the really smart animals, and I want to see how dolphins compare," Wally explained. "Some say dolphins are smarter. I have to find one really smart dolphin; that's what counts for me."

Mo Wintermantel kept his aspirations to himself. He was shorter than Wally, about average height, and more muscular. He walked on slightly bowed legs with a well-balanced spring, like a small hunting animal. Mo told me he had been reared on an Iowa farm and had been in the navy aboard an aircraft carrier during World War II. After the war he took up fishing and spent several summers in Alaska hauling in salmon, mending nets, and repairing gear. Later he went to work for an aquarium—still fishing but bringing his prey back alive for the exhibits. At POP he had developed a technique for capturing dolphins in the Catalina Channel, west of Santa Monica.

POP, which has since closed, had two large concrete dolphin tanks, each about sixty feet in diameter and twelve feet deep. One tank contained a pair of white-striped dolphins like the one I had autopsied at Point Mugu. These were "Lags," as I learned to call them, a nickname based on their scientific name, *Lagenorhynchus obliquidens.* In the other large tank, adjacent to a grandstand for spectators, were two trained Atlantic bottlenosed dolphins named Lana and Toro.

As we approached the tank, Lana and Toro came over to the side, dancing on broad tail flukes and looking up at us with open mouths. These were the first bottlenosed dolphins I had met, and a chill down my spine registered my excitement in their eager presence. "We have a performance coming up in a few minutes," Wally said. "Mo can take you up to the grandstand to see the show better."

As Mo and I watched from the bleachers, I could see that the female dolphin, Lana, was well trained. Wally had taught her to jump high in the air to take fish; she leaped through hoops, put her snout through a ring attached to a towline to pull a small boat around the tank, and treaded water by the pool's edge, extending a flipper so humans could reach out and shake hands (or flippers, depending on your point of view).

The male dolphin was less cooperative. "Toro is a freeloader," said Mo, pointing toward the big dolphin, who stayed beside the feeding station, looking up at Wally with an open mouth. Each time Lana returned to the station to receive a handful of fish chunks as a reward, Toro rasped and bleated, demanding food for himself. The single cube of mackerel that Wally pitched immediately disappeared into Toro's constantly open mouth.

After the show we walked back to poolside, where Wally was standing. As we talked we were distracted by Lana, who had eased her forebody over the tank rim to poke the shiny steel fish container on Wally's belt. "If the navy wants to study porpoises, they should work with this kind," said Mo, reaching out to pat Lana's head. He smiled. "You see, they're gray like everything else the navy has."

Back at Point Mugu, I reported to Dr. Hall, telling him about my visit to the sea circus. "I'm glad you met those fellows," he said. "Things are working out now, so I can tell you that we are working on a contract with Wally and Mo. They own five bottlenosed dolphins that they caught some time ago down in Mississippi. Their problem is that the dolphins are in Mississippi and they can't afford to fly them out to California. If I can wangle a navy plane to fly them, we can have two of those dolphins for our project."

"I'll keep my fingers crossed," I said.

As I drove home that evening, I was anxious to tell Jeanette about all my new experiences with dolphins. I knew that Dr. Hall was trying to work it out so a job would be available for me. Maybe, I thought elatedly, I would become a dolphin doctor.

My dolphin education began in earnest a few days after my first trip to Pacific Ocean Park. On a cold, foggy spring morning about four months before we first met Tuffy, Wally picked me up at 3 A.M. for a dolphin hunt. To reach my home, Wally had traveled from his home in Thousand Oaks, California, where he lived with a kennel and a menagerie of animals, including, occasionally, an elephant. We planned to drive from my house in Camarillo to Santa Monica, where we would meet Mo and board their vessel.

Highway 1, the coastal route, was familiar to me, but I was not prepared for our mode of travel, a green Crosley pickup. The bed of Wally's little truck was big enough for the bale of hay that sat in it but not much more. To a man of my considerable bulk, the passenger seat hardly looked comfortable. To get into the cab beside Wally, I had to crouch down and pull my knees almost to my chest. As we drove away, I asked Wally why he had such a small pickup. He mumbled something about good gas mileage and trailed off into a wide yawn. I gathered that at such an early hour Wally did not want to discuss his pickup or anything else.

About 4:30 A.M., a good half-hour later than our promised arrival, we finally reached Mo's place. He was out front surrounded by a large pile of paraphernalia: pipes, poles, hoops, a thermos, a strongbox, a carton of groceries, a large roll of foam rubber, something that looked like a cage for a very large fat squirrel, and miscellaneous small items.

Without a word of greeting Mo began loading the gear into the bed of the trucklet. He packed the groceries and the thermos in the rear, behind the bale of hay, but he needed help with the strongbox. Both Mo and Wally pushed with all their might against the bale of hay to wedge the box in alongside. I tried to imagine a use for the hay—wet hay for padding dolphins? Working men did not want idle questions from novices, I thought. Surely the normal passage of events would reveal the hay's purpose. Mo and Wally draped lengths of rope over the load and tied them under the truck, cinching them tighter and tighter until I imagined the little truck groaning like an overburdened mule.

The only things left to pack were two poles and two pipes with hoops attached. Each was longer than the vehicle. Wally got into the driver's seat, and Mo positioned the poles above Wally's outside rearview mirror, tying them in back and at the mirror. I noticed that this arrangement prevented the opening of the door on the driver's side, and we still had two more pipes and hoops to deal with. I guessed that Mo would pack them in the same way against the opposite side of the vehicle, and I wondered when that was done how we were going to get inside the truck.

Mo attached one end of the pair of pipes to the rear of the truck with rubber tubing. He motioned for me to get into the cab, and I pushed up against Wally, who sat under the steering wheel, pinned to the opposite door. Mo performed a juggling act with the pipes and the passenger door, which got him inside the truck with the pipes in his hand outside the window. Despite his efforts, however, Mo couldn't close the door. Repeating his maneuver and trying the reverse hand order, he still could not even get close. I lifted myself as much as possible and rotated to the right so I could reach across with my left hand and help Mo close the door. With a mighty heave we both got it closed, but our confinement brought grunts and labored respiration from Wally, who was now behind and slightly under me, out of reach of the gear shift.

"Look," I said, "I'm the biggest. Somehow there is always more room if I sit next to the door." Mo dropped the pipes, which clattered noisily to the pavement. After some effort to reach the door handle he managed to exit. As I followed, I heard Wally release a deep breath.

Mo got back in. Before reboarding the Crosley, I removed my heavy jacket and tied it to the hoop at the forward end of a pipe. In the Crosley's headlights, my coat looked like a bearskin stretched out to dry with its arms dangling. Repeating the maneuver I had seen Mo do earlier with the pipes, I succeeded in closing the door. The little pickup moved forward as Wally steered and Mo shifted gears. I watched my coat out front, straining water from the dense, foggy air as we crept along slick, dark pavement toward the harbor. When the Crosley stopped, water dribbled from my coat, forming a puddle on the dock.

All three of us gathered as much equipment as we could carry and headed for the boat. At low tide, the boat was about twelve feet below the level of the dock, and we had to hand things down a ladder. After carrying two loads and hanging my wet coat on the mast, I left Mo and Wally sorting the gear on deck and returned to the pickup for the bale of hay, which was all that remained. Having had experience with hay, I hoisted the eighty-pound bale, carrying it in a professional manner that I hoped would be recognized and praised. Mo and Wally were fully consumed with preparations for the trip, however, and took no notice when I arrived on the dock above the boat.

I put down the bale of hay to catch my breath and study the situation. Ladders often caused me trouble, but I decided that if I put the hay on my shoulder as I climbed down the ladder and let the bale lean against the dock, I could get it on board without disturbing Wally and Mo. Backing down the ladder, pulling the bale over the side to let it rest on my shoulder, I carefully reached with my foot for a lower step, allowing the hay to slide down; then I rested for the next move. As I reached for a lower step, I was startled by a sudden shout.

"Doc, stop!"

The last time I heard such a sound was when someone in my Boy Scout troop was about to step on a rattlesnake. I froze in place.

"Doc, what the hell are you going to do with that bale of hay?" growled Mo.

"Put it back," yelled Wally. "We don't need it here!"

I pushed on the bale, now pinned at an angle between my shoulder and the dock. My method was practical for going down but not for climbing back up. I needed help. Mo climbed the ladder, and as he reached around from behind to help me maneuver the bale, he scolded Wally standing on the boat deck below.

"Why don't you ever clean out that sorry little pickup?" he said. "You're always carrying around a bale of hay or a dog kennel or something you don't need that just gets in the way."

As we got the bale onto the dock, the humor of the situation seemed to dawn on Wally. He slapped his thighs and laughed. "Hey, Doc, did you think we were going to hunt elephants?" he teased. "Leave it there, Doc. Nobody around here is going to steal a bale of hay."

I worried that such an inauspicious beginning would mar the trip, but Mo and Wally were kind. As we traveled through the Catalina Channel, we all speculated about the various ways one could use a bale of hay on a dolphin hunt. Our merriment lasted until noon, but after the long morning, our spirits sank. We had not yet seen a single dolphin or pilot whale, or even a sea lion. The sea was calm but clothed in thick fog. We could see no more than a quarter of a mile on either side of the boat. "I thought the fog would burn off by noon," Mo said plaintively.

While we peered through the murk trying to spot dolphins, I asked Mo about his technique for capturing these mammals. As far as Mo knew, only three or four other men had developed methods for taking dolphins alive in the open sea, and each kept the means secret; therefore, Mo had to devise his own technique. His method relied on the playful nature of dolphins, which often ride the bow waves created by a moving craft, like surfers riding a wave near the beach. Capitalizing on this behavior, Mo constructed a small portable pulpit (the gadget that looked like a squirrel cage) to extend from the bow of the capture boat. Carrying the device with him the way a cowboy carries a saddle, Mo had it ready to hook on any boat that happened to be available. The pulpit extended over the bow wave so Mo could look down on the dolphins and be in a good position to try to snare one with his hoop net.

The hoop net, about three feet in diameter, was attached to the end of a sturdy pipe about twelve feet long. A netting bag about four feet long, with a rope noose built into the opening, hung from the hoop like an oversized butterfly net. The drawstring noose that closed the bag extended in a coil of about one hundred feet of rope to a buoy, which would mark the position of a netted dolphin.

As we cruised through flat seas with no sign of dolphins, Mo's hoop net lay ready on deck. When the fog lifted, sunlight shining through clouds lit the ocean with bright yellow patches of fire. Suddenly we spotted a large herd of dolphins. "Lags," Mo called. "A thousand."

Wally corrected him. "At least two thousand."

Dark blue dorsal fins broke the surface in clusters as far as we could see. Dolphins swam this way and that, crisscrossing through each other's wake. "Feeding on anchovies," Mo explained. "These fellows probably won't play."

Wally slowed the boat to about five knots. After about ten minutes, one dolphin finally showed up on our bow. Then there was another and another, and then at least ten dolphins were surfing across the bow, just under my position on the deck. With his capture net poised only an arm's length above the water, Mo stood almost motionless in his pulpit. With the hoop he tracked the dolphins' movements back and forth.

Lying on the deck, I held the buoy and rope in my left hand, ready to throw them into the wave. Under the bow, the water was crystal clear. I could not keep track of all the dolphins, even though I strained to follow them skimming on the bow wave. Phantoms appeared far below our boat, rising out of the hazy blue depths like white puffs of smoke. Their ghostly figures remained for a minute or two and then vanished in the deep.

Making long leaps in unison like well-trained teams of horses, other dolphins came along the surface. Dolphins were continuously on the bow, sweeping back and forth, turning from one side to the other. Sometimes they nipped each other on the tail or traded slaps of the fluke. I was thrilled by the beauty of their natural ballet.

Almost directly below me a large dolphin swam accompanied by one only a third its size. Sticking close by its mother's side, the calf scarcely seemed to move its little flukes and flippers. The mother stroked her tail now and then to keep them in position. Obviously, the pair rode the boat's wave, using little of their own power. An instant later, down they both went, moving together as if tied by an invisible cord. The mother pumped her flukes fast. Just as the boat's bow wave had carried the dolphins, I reasoned, the mother's wave now carried the calf beside her.

I was fascinated, but after about an hour of watching these dolphins Mo decided to break off and look for another herd. "Too many mothers and calves with this bunch," Mo said. "We don't want to catch a mother or a calf, and you can't always tell which dolphins are mothers when they act like this."

Another hour passed, and we saw no other dolphins. Since it was getting late, Wally decided we should turn for port, but we still kept our eyes open for any sign of dolphins. "Look for collections of flying sea birds, splashes, white water, or anything dark on the surface," Mo said. "That's where you'll find dolphins."

The sun was low when Mo spotted one of these signs and asked Wally to turn the boat. As we peered across the waves, we saw large, black, rounded dorsal fins break the surface. "Pilot whales," said Mo.

Wally took us on a run through the herd of pilot whales, just for a look. The whales swam slowly, seeming to pay little attention to us as they alternately appeared above the waves to blow and then dive again. "Pilot whales don't ride the bow," Mo said. "We'll have to figure out some other way to catch them."

I happened to look down and spotted a dolphin on our bow wave. "Hey, Mo, there's a Lag!"

"Where?"

"Right down here on the bow."

Mo grabbed his hoop net and jumped into the pulpit. I took my position behind him, ready to throw the buoy. Almost motionless on our wave just to the left of the bow, the Lag seemed to watch us with its large, dark right eye. The animal tilted up directly under Mo's pulpit and broke the surface to breathe. "Be ready," said Mo. "The next time he does that, I'm going to bag him."

Wally kept the boat going straight ahead at constant speed. The dolphin continued its leisurely ride on the bow wave. When the animal tilted back and moved forward slightly, Mo plunged the net down. I threw the buoy, and the rope snaked out. But the dolphin was quicker, and it turned its head to the left just enough to avoid going through the net. "Just bumped him on the snout," Mo said as he hurried out of the pulpit, his hoop net sagging in disarray.

The dolphin was still there just below our feet. It seemed to be watching our flurry of activity with great interest, and I thought it must be either laughing at our awkwardness or begging to be caught. I pulled in the rope and buoy as fast as possible while Mo got his spare hoop ready. By now, the dolphin had surfed on our bow for at least five minutes. Mo was waiting for the moment when it would have to surface again to breathe.

As the dolphin broke the surface, Mo jammed the hoop squarely in front of it, and the animal slipped cleanly into the net. I tossed the buoy, and the rope payed out. Wally turned the boat toward the left, the side the dolphin was on, and cut the engines to idle. The boat bobbed slowly up and down on the glassy swell.

The pilot whales were nowhere to be seen, nor was the dolphin. The net, the rope, and the buoy also had vanished, but Mo did not seem overly concerned. He looked at his watch. "He's been down two minutes. He'll be up pretty soon." He paused. "Unless we've lost him."

Another minute passed in the gathering dusk. The engine coughed to a stop, and the only sounds were the slow creak of our boat as it rose on the swell and the water dripping off first one end, then the other as the boat tilted.

"There! Over there!" yelled Mo.

Wally started the engine. Now I could see the large, dented yellow buoy. "He went deep," said Mo, as he took up a long boat hook. Wally maneuvered the craft to the buoy, which was bobbing away from us like a runaway fishing cork. Mo snared the buoy with his hook, lifted it on board, and handed it to me. "Keep taking in the slack," he said. "Walk him back to the stern."

Now I could see the dolphin clearly. It seemed confused and was pulling straight ahead, pumping its flukes and blowing, with the net wrapped around its forebody. Mo put on his wet suit top and jumped in to maneuver the dolphin into a lifting sling. As he took hold of the dolphin around its midsection, the animal protested. The flukes moved more quickly, and the dolphin tossed its head from side to side like a young horse trying to throw off a halter. Gradually the dolphin's objections subsided, and Mo pulled the animal toward the stern.

By the time we delivered the newly captured dolphin to a large tank at POP, it was nearly midnight. I gladly accepted a ride home from Dr. Robert Miller, the POP consulting veterinarian, who had come down from Ventura County to see the new animal. Mo told me later that he sold the Lag we captured to an oceanarium in the Netherlands. I never did learn whether Wally got his bale of hay back.

Over the years Mo caught several more Lags, including two that eventually resided in the main pool at Point Mugu. These dolphins, captured only a mile or two from Mugu Rock, had swum with the herds of

Lags that we often spotted seaward of the dolphin pools at the base. When we began training Tuffy in the ocean there, I wondered what would happen when he encountered these exuberant dolphins in the wild. Would he join the free wild herd or would he return to his trainer's call?

My veterinary work with live dolphins started four months later, the day I met Tuffy, a bottlenosed dolphin. It all began when I received an unexpected summons as I conducted a routine clinic at Oxnard Air Force Base. The waiting room that day was crowded with German shepherds excited by the presence of fellow canines. This waiting room actually was a battered Quonset hut of World War II vintage that stood in a corner of the motor pool parking lot. Although the structure was humble, its floor was buffed to a high shine, the walls were well painted, and the stainless steel and glass appurtenances of the clinic gleamed. They were kept this way because they were under the supervision of Senior Master Sergeant Jesse Haggins, a man of mild manner who suddenly became tyrannical when the enlisted men made any breach of his standard of cleanliness or order. The sergeant strictly controlled access to the clinic, seeing to it that I was not disturbed when I was attending animal patients. I was surprised, therefore, when my examination of Wolf, our largest and most menacing sentry dog, was interrupted. I glanced down past Wolf's intimidating eyes to see my face reflected in Sergeant Haggins's polished shoes.

"Captain Ridgway," he said, "the base control tower

is on the telephone. They have an urgent message for you."

I couldn't imagine why the tower would have an urgent message for me. On an air force base, the tower speaks only to pilots in airplanes and flight commanders on the ground. Maybe there was a sick sentry dog at a missile site, and they wanted me to fly up. Or maybe there was food poisoning somewhere. But why would the message come from the tower?

"Captain Ridgway?"

"Yes."

"This is Oxnard Tower. We have a message from an incoming navy C-121 bound for the air station at Point Mugu. They are carrying five live dolphins with an estimated time of arrival at 1630. They request that a veterinarian be on hand at touchdown."

"Tell them I will be there," I said.

The plane would land in an hour. We finished with Wolf and sent him back to the kennel. Then I went to my office to check my emergency bag, trying to think of everything I might need to treat a sick or injured dolphin. "This is the chance you've been waiting for," I told myself. "Don't muff it." During the short drive to Point Mugu, I tried to remember what I had learned about dolphins. My knowledge seemed woefully incomplete.

On the tarmac at Point Mugu, I watched the four propellers of the Constellation jerk to a halt. The twin orange-tipped tail stood high above the parking apron. An odd yellow truck on small, fat wheels rolled under the tail and backed up to the side of the plane. With some belching of smoke the truck lifted a wide platform to the open aircraft door. I climbed up through the door to face some curious looks. There were questions about my air force uniform and large black bag. I soon saw the familiar faces of Wally, Mo, and Bill Scronce, who assured the navy men that, despite my suspicious appearance, I was an expert and was there to help.

The navy men prepared to off-load the dolphins. The big fish, as I silently labeled them at the time, lay almost inert on thick mattresses attached to wooden pallets. Only parts of their gray heads were exposed. Moist bed sheets covered their bodies from eyes to tail. Every twenty or thirty seconds the U-shaped slit at the top of each gray head opened, like a small child's mouth agape. Watching the dolphins closely, I noticed that with each exhalation the body seemed to sink, then quickly rise as the animal inhaled. Their breathing seemed labored. How could I tell which of these creatures was sick?

Using garden sprayers, the attendants kept the dolphins wet as they moved them along the metal floor toward the large cargo door I had entered. Sailors scooted the first dolphin onto the yellow platform, then lowered it to a gray navy truck. I was amazed that these large, powerful animals, so swift and active in the water, could be so still.

"Have they been tranquilized?" I asked Wally.

"No, we haven't given them anything," he said. "You're the doctor."

Wally told me he was concerned about one female, which breathed more rapidly than the other dolphins, appeared restless during the trip, and had some swollen skin sores. Wally asked the sailors to put this distressed dolphin on the truck beside the first animal. When this was done, the truck moved a short distance away so another truck could move into position to collect the remaining animals. Wally stayed in the plane to help finish the unloading, sending me down to the truck to examine my patients.

I pressed my stethoscope against one dolphin's chest, while people crowded around to observe my exam. The press of the crowd made me uncomfortable. I didn't relish such close scrutiny on my first attempt to examine and treat a live dolphin. Some people regard it as criminal to take these animals from the wild, I thought uneasily. But as I went on with my work, I found the crowd to be friendly. They were navy men in dungarees, officers in khaki, and brightly dressed women and children who had come to greet their husbands and fathers.

"Are they as intelligent as I hear they are?" asked one lady.

"Yes. I understand that dolphins are very intelligent," I said.

"Do they bite?" asked a young boy.

"No, they don't bite people, just fish and sharks," I said.

The dolphins lay motionless, except that every half-minute their blowholes opened and their chests contracted. After hearing a pair of clear breaths about thirty seconds apart, I heard something unusual: choking or gasping. The healthy-looking dolphin next to the one with the skin sores arched its back and slapped its tail against the supporting mattress. Trying to get a better look, I yanked the bed sheet covering the animal with a forceful tug, unexpectedly pulling about six inches of the sheet out of the dolphin's blowhole. The animal took a deep breath and then another. It looked toward me, snorted, and opened its mouth threateningly. It seemed to stare directly at me with its right eye. As I raised the sheet farther to get it out of harm's way, I noticed a large crescent scar on the dolphin's right side.

I let the moist sheet drop around the dolphin's tail and returned to the sick dolphin to prepare an antibiotic injection. More people crowded around. Trying to look as if I knew what I was doing, I lifted the sheet, patted the side of the gray body, and washed the smooth skin with alcohol. As my needle pierced the skin, I noticed that neither the alcohol nor the needle brought more than a mild jerk from my patient. The gaze of the other dolphin seemed welded to me, but its body did not move. The injection should keep the infection from spreading, I thought. I can examine the animals more thoroughly later, after they have a chance to rest in their seawater pool.

Wally pushed through the crowd to see what I was doing. When I told him about the problem with the bed sheet, he was concerned. "We've been minding these animals steadily for twelve hours," he groaned. "It would be a shame to lose one from choking on a sheet."

"This fellow has been through a lot," I said, pointing to the large crescent-shaped scar I had seen on the dolphin's side. "What do you suppose caused that scar?"

"It must have been a shark three times his size to make a mark like that," Wally replied. "He must have had a rough life in the ocean. I've never seen so many scars on such a small porpoise."

Until a new pumping system was completed at the dolphin pool at Point Mugu, Wally and Mo temporarily kept all the dolphins at Pacific Ocean Park in Santa Monica. Later in the week I drove to POP to examine them. All the dolphins were swimming together in a tight circle near the middle of a large pool. Mo had lowered the water level so the dolphins could be caught easily and isolated for my medical examination, and their response was to bunch together in the center of the tank. To attract their attention I reached over and slapped the inner edge of the tank wall. Closing formation, the animals continued circling together counterclockwise. I slapped the wall again, this time making a louder noise. The dolphin with the crescent scar broke away from the others, widened its circle slightly, and eyed me momentarily from about ten feet away.

"That's the one that almost choked on the sheet," said Wally. "He's thinner than the rest and has that big scar. All the others are eating a few fish each day, but this one won't even look at food."

As I waited for the large pool to empty, I watched the animals. The more I saw of these creatures with their inquiring gazes, the more they aroused my curiosity. My first interest in dolphins had been strictly medical—another mammal to learn about and to join the many other mammals in my library of veterinary knowledge. But as I watched the dolphins and saw them looking back with their large dark eyes, I thought I understood why ancient storytellers and modern writers alike usually romanticized the dolphin. Certain beliefs often are repeated. I had read that dolphins are friends of man, cooperate with fishermen, attack and kill sharks by ramming them, save drowning swimmers, and never bite or harm humans. Since such viewpoints seemed to be poorly documented, I wondered how much truth was in them.

As the water ebbed from the tank, the dolphins were left in a much smaller pool about twenty feet wide, inset in the bottom of the larger tank. This pool was only three feet deep, and the smooth concrete floor of the drained tank made a handy examination area. Our plan was to remove the dolphins one at a time and to place each on a foam-rubber pad next to the inner tank, cushioning the animal and making it as comfortable as possible during my examination.

Because these dolphins weighed two hundred to three hundred pounds each, it took several brawny helpers to catch, lift, and hold the animals. Mo, Marty, and Bill Scronce donned wet suits, and Wally pulled on his waist-length, one-piece rubber trousers and boots. As the examination progressed, the four men caught the dolphins one at a time and laid each in its turn on the thick foam-rubber mattress. I went about the medical examination much the same way I would have for any other animal. First I looked in the mouth and checked the skin. Then I put in a rectal thermometer for a temperature measurement, attaching two feet of nylon thread so I could retrieve the instrument if it slipped in too far. My "safety line" was based on a standard procedure used in the examination of horses and cows, since the animal might shift suddenly or strain at any time. From analyzing the postmortem at Point Mugu and from reading published papers, I had deduced that the dolphin's internal anatomy was similar in some ways to that of a cow. I also had learned that dolphins were susceptible to erysipelas, a swine disease. It seemed only logical to me that I should rely on my experience with livestock.

With farm animals veterinarians are concerned about pneumonia following long trips such as the one these dolphins had just made; therefore, I listened with my stethoscope to the chest of each dolphin. I treated skin sores with an antiseptic blue dye that stained the sores and would not wash off in the water. On a human, such sores would have been bandaged, but to bandage a dolphin is impractical; nothing will stick to its skin for more than a few hours. I nicked the dorsal fin with a razor blade, collecting a few drops of blood in a capillary tube. From this I could tell, among other things, if the dolphins were anemic or if the white blood cell count was elevated because of infection, although at that time there was little data on normal dolphins by which to assess the tests. I gave each dolphin vitamin injections, since the animals were not yet eating as much as they should have and some of them had ulcers around their teeth. I had been told that Dr. Miller had diagnosed scurvy in dolphins here the past spring, so I was especially concerned that the animals not be vitamin deficient.

As the last procedure, I pulled out the thermometer and read the temperature. I didn't know what was normal for a dolphin, but these all registered around 98 degrees Fahrenheit. When I finished with each dolphin, my helpers carefully placed the animal back in the shallow water with the others. Wally, clad in his rubber overalls and boots, waded around the gray dorsal fins until he could point out an animal we had not yet treated; then he supervised our crew in catching the next animal from the tight group. In the murky water it was not easy to tell one dolphin from another.

I was almost finished. Wally pointed to the only dolphin left to examine—the skinny one with the crescent-shaped scar. First, Mo grabbed the animal around the chest just behind the flippers. Then Bill and Marty latched onto the tail behind the dorsal fin, Unexpectedly, the dolphin recoiled. With its snout it swatted Mo on the head, knocking him backward into the pool. With its tail flukes the dolphin flailed Marty's shins and knocked him headlong into the water. Bill received several body blows in the melee and disappeared briefly under the churning murk. The aggrieved dolphin rushed past Wally, knocking him into the water.

While all this was going on in the small pool, I stood on the concrete ledge, busily arranging my medical gear for the next examination. As waves of water generated by the commotion lapped across my work space, I moved my gear farther away from the pool's edge. Uncertainly, I stood back, wondering whether I should try to help or just keep out of the way. After taking one look at the recovering crew, I decided the latter course was wiser.

Mo bobbed up, sputtering and coughing. Wally, looking totally disgusted, was draining his rubber suit; full of water, the overalls weighed about three hundred pounds, making it impossible for him to walk. Bill was on his way out of the tank to call for reinforcements.

Soon another stout fellow arrived to help, and I joined the catching group. About ten minutes of thrashes, splashes, bites, and bruises followed. Finally, the skinny dolphin with the scar lay still on the rubber pad with four men draped across it. I hurriedly gave the vitamin injection and inserted the thermometer. I rushed to complete my treatment as soon as possible.

"Almost finished," I thought with some relief. I

reached to retrieve the rectal thermometer. I couldn't feel it, so I reached again. No luck. It was gone. Only an inch of string protruded from the dolphin. As I grasped for the string, the dolphin gave another great heave and overpowered the tail-holders. Knowing that if the dolphin flopped off the mat it could injure itself, I threw the full weight of my body across its tail, and we tried to hold it on the mat. When we finally restrained the dolphin, I again reached for the string. This time, however, both thermometer and string had disappeared. The wretched animal had sucked up not only my thermometer but all two feet of safety line as well.

When I inserted my finger into the dolphin's rectum to fish for the string, the dolphin clapped its jaws together and began a rasping, screeching, scolding sound. It wiggled and squirmed, bit, and jumped free of our grasp, flouncing across the smooth concrete until it regained the small pool and fell into the water.

The men stood around somewhat dazed for a moment. They were beaten to a frazzle. Fat lips, bloody noses, torn clothing, and too many bruises to count proved that the dolphin had shown us who was boss. After a brief discussion all the men agreed that we could not go back for my thermometer. "He's likely to pass it," I said, mostly to reassure myself. "There's danger only if it should be broken."

"We'll keep an eye on him and let you know," huffed Wally. Then, struck by the spectacle of our crew battered by a single dolphin, he laughed. "Anyway, we have a name for that dolphin with the shark-bite scar. From now on he's Tough Guy." He took a dripping little notebook from his breast pocket and wrote the words "Tuf Guy."

The next morning I telephoned Wally at POP to find out how the dolphins were doing and to ask whether my thermometer had turned up. "No sign of your thermometer," Wally answered, "but Tuf Guy is eating today. He took fifteen pounds of mackerel first thing this morning. Maybe all that wrestling we did yesterday gave him an appetite."

Wally hung up. I had learned to come to the point quickly in any telephone conversation with Wally. He never said hello or good-bye; when he was through talking, he would just hang up.

When I completed active duty at Oxnard Air Force Base at the end of October 1962, Dr. Lee Hall hired me as full-time "animal health officer" for the Naval Missile Center at Point Mugu. This position was a temporary one that was to be renewed at the end of the year. I was to look after the dolphins used in research at Point Mugu directed by Dr. William McLean of the Naval Ordnance Test Station (NOTS), a laboratory on the Mojave Desert at China Lake, California, about 130 miles inland. (Dr. McLean had invented the Sidewinder missile, among other achievements. It was largely because of his great prestige in the navy that our "far-out" dolphin project could get support.) Dr. McLean was intrigued by the neuroscientist Dr. John Lilly's ideas about dolphin intelligence, but there also were many practical reasons for the navy to study dolphins.

In 1960 navy scientists at Marineland near Los Angeles had started training a Pacific white-sided dolphin named Notty for speed runs designed to learn how the dolphin could swim so fast; the navy hoped to apply what it learned to torpedo and ship designs. The scientists posed many questions about how dolphins coped so well in the sea. After some months of study, however, more questions than answers had accumulated. They were still not sure whether they could perform swimming tests to measure the speed of untethered animals. They also wondered how to measure the effectiveness of dolphin sonar and, indeed, whether something could be learned from dolphin sonar that would improve navy sonar. One of their more persistent questions concerned the possibility of training dolphins to assist navy divers in undersea tasks.

Notty was one of the dolphins that had sickened and died before I became involved with the project. Since they had learned so much from this dolphin, navy scientists resolved to continue their research. To that end they built the small facility for keeping dolphins at Point Mugu Naval Base, next to a large seawater lagoon opening into the Pacific Ocean. But the three dolphins brought to Point Mugu during that first summer died. My autopsy of the last one led to my present job.

I had been at work only a short time when Dr. Rene Engle, who looked a little and spoke a lot like Albert Einstein, arrived at Point Mugu from NOTS headquarters at China Lake. He intended to initiate us in dolphin science. By that time Bob Bailey, a young UCLA graduate, had been hired as head dolphin trainer. One important ingredient for Bob's work was still missing, however: There were no dolphins at Point Mugu.

The lack of dolphins was only temporary, however,

because soon we were to receive two of the dolphins housed at Pacific Ocean Park. Wally still owned Tuf Guy and the four other unnamed dolphins the navy had transported from Mississippi. According to the deal Dr. Hall and Wally had struck, the navy could have first pick of the dolphins. Wally would select the second one from the group of five, then the navy would take another dolphin from the three remaining animals.

Bob and I were appointed to select the two dolphins for the navy. "Try to get one of each sex," Dr. Engle told us. "We should name them Dot and Dash as the signal for the letter A in the Morse code." I assumed that these names had some significance, perhaps to the scientific study of dolphin communication. It was clear to me that the selection process would pit two greenhorns, Bob and me, against that old horse trader, elephant swapper, and dolphin trickster Wally Ross. But the prospect of dolphin-dealing with Wally did not worry me as much as the other event at POP scheduled for that day. I had been informed that the admiral in charge of Point Mugu was to attend a meeting in Los Angeles, and if he had time, he planned to drop by POP in nearby Santa Monica to see the navy's new dolphins. This news was a bit disconcerting because I had never met an admiral and Dr. Hall had appointed me to explain the dolphins to this imposing officer.

I was still practicing a short speech for the admiral when Bob and I arrived at the park. "Is he going to select the navy dolphins?" Wally asked when I told him about the important visitor we expected.

"No, I think he just wants to see them," I replied. Wally agreed to have the female bottlenosed dolphin, Lana, do some jumps and tricks and shake hands so the admiral could see how agile, clever, and trainable dolphins are.

No sooner had these arrangements been made than the admiral arrived with his aide and a couple of other officers. I ushered the group onto the viewing ramp between pools. The dull-gray bottlenosed dolphins were on the left, adjacent to a tank containing three striking Pacific white-striped dolphins that Mo recently had captured. I motioned toward the bottlenosed dolphins and after clearing my throat declared with as impressive a tone as I could summon, "The navy dolphins are in this tank, Admiral."

The admiral seemed a bit unimpressed. "Of course those are the navy dolphins," he replied. "The rascals are gray, aren't they?"

This old joke brought a great chuckle from his entourage. Wally just smiled. As for me, my speech about bottlenosed dolphins ran aground, a wreck before it ever got started. But since Lana performed her part of the show flawlessly, the admiral left his brief tour with a good impression—of the animals, at least.

After the admiral's departure, Bob and I turned to the business of selecting dolphins. As far as I was concerned, Tuf Guy was out. I was not eager to repeat a roughhouse incident like the one with the thermometer. In addition, we all had noticed that Tuf Guy had scars and some areas of unhealthy skin. "If he were a horse," I told Bob, "I'd reject him on scars, if nothing else." Bob nodded in solemn agreement. Naively, I took Wally's broad smile as a sign of his approval.

Instead, Bob and I selected the youngest male, a smooth little dolphin of two hundred pounds that had few marks or blemishes. Although Wally said nothing, our selection seemed to please him. Following Dr.

Engle's instructions, we called the animal Dash. Wally picked a young female, leaving us with a difficult decision. Reluctantly, we chose the only remaining female, a large dolphin with many skin sores. We named her Dot, again according to Dr. Engle's suggestion.

Even though Dot and Dash were now the official property of the navy, we continued to house the two dolphins at POP until the water supply pumps in the tanks at Point Mugu were finished. Finding pneumonia in the last dolphin to die at Point Mugu, I had concluded that insufficient water flow to the main pool might have resulted in an exaggerated growth of harmful bacteria. I had recommended the installation of pumps at the end of Mugu Pier, which would bring six hundred gallons of ocean water per minute through our dolphin pools.

The installation of this improved water system caused a temporary delay in our studies, since we had no dolphins at Point Mugu and it was difficult to work at POP. Meanwhile, Dr. Engle, our interim leader, induced Bob, Marty, Bill Scronce, and me to practice animal training procedures. "Use chickens," Dr. Engle recommended. "Whoever cannot train a chicken, cannot train."

Though educated in physics, Dr. Engle was a superb apologist for animal psychology. To acquaint us with animal training methods, he persuaded this bunch of tough sailors and cranky civilians to spend a whole day teaching a chicken to dance. Dr. Engle's instruction had the air of profound wisdom. For example, he would ask us, "When a porpoise comes over to you, what does he want?" Then he himself would answer the question, intoning solemnly, "Feedback, that's what he wants." None of us talked back to our eminent teacher, but I think the general sentiment was that after a few hours of "chicken dance school," we were more than ready to work with dolphins. But we had to wait.

I still had plenty of veterinary work at POP, where I went frequently to check our two dolphins. I found that Dash appeared to be adjusting well to his habitat and companions. Dot, the female, was another matter. She moved slowly and ate sparingly. To coax her to eat, we offered her food five or six times a day, encouraging her to take all of her basic ration of fifteen pounds of fish. We were worried. Dot was losing weight along her tail, beside the dorsal fin, and forward of the flippers. Equally troubling were the increasing number of pustules that appeared on her skin.

I was trying to give the dolphins the best care possible, but something still seemed to be lacking. I began giving Dot antibiotic capsules placed inside fish, but she was finicky. We learned to wait until she seemed willing to swallow another fish, then pitch the medicated one into her mouth. Swallowing fish whole, the dolphin did not seem to notice the capsules.

Checking Dot carefully, I noticed that her teeth were worn and flattened. This reminded me of something I had seen in an aged horse I once treated in Texas. The horse lived on sandy soil where grass was sparse. As many years passed, the sand in his daily ration of grass wore his teeth right down to the gum. The similar condition of Dot's teeth indicated that she was very old.

We worked with Dot for three months, but despite our best efforts, the dolphin became progressively weaker and finally died. In the autopsy we found a green bacteria in her tissues known to cause abscesses and pneumonia in humans and other mammals. Dot's death troubled me, not only because I was sorry to lose a dolphin but also because I worried that her condition presented a pattern that might be repeated with other animals. I knew I must find ways to prevent this.

About a month after Dot's death our water system at Point Mugu was completed, and we were ready to move Dash. Marty and Bill put a six-inch-thick foam-rubber mattress in the bed of the pickup truck, and next to it they placed a large can of water and a garden sprayer so we could keep Dash moist and cool during the return trip. Bob and Bill cheerfully piled into the bed of the pickup and leaned back for a windy ride in the sunshine. I climbed into the cab with Marty. Since Marty was usually in no mood to converse while he was driving the curving shore highway, I leaned back to enjoy the coastal scenery and to reminisce.

Coastal Route 1 hugs the beach past Mugu Rock and winds its way along the breaking surf through Malibu and into Santa Monica, where Pacific Ocean Park was located. Although by this time I had lived in California for more than two years, I was in many ways still an inland Texas boy dazzled by his first encounter with the Pacific Ocean and its creatures. When I was a boy walking over the parched earth of South Texas, where my father raised cattle, sheep, and other livestock, I had no idea, not even a dream, of the mammals that ranged the sea. Instead, I was concerned with creatures of the land, which ranged the wide pastures where hot summer winds blew clouds of dust. These animals were both my chore and my frustration. Yet as I was to discover in later years, my experiences with sheep and other livestock prepared me in some ways for my future career.

In my boyhood, as I walked before the dusty, unshorn sheep led by Old Goat, my daydreams often led me to other places. These flights of fancy were almost always connected to my consuming interests at the time: history and football. I dreamed of the landslide election: Sam Ridgway, U.S. senator. In my fantasy, people stood up to cheer when I came through our small town of Devine, and children ran up to me pleading for my autograph. Soon, most times, the calls of these imaginary children faded into the sustained roar of a crowd as, breaking through a phalanx of hard, muscular bodies, Sam Ridgway, all-American quarterback, made a touchdown.

At such times Old Goat would grow impatient with my slackened gait and jab me with his stumpy horns. Little did his nudging bring me back to reality, however. Instead, it became the jolt of my bronco as I lunged into the dusty rodeo arena. The announcer's voice grew louder as Bronco Bustin' Ridgway, urged by the cheering crowd, held his seat on the pitching horse. One hand in the air for balance, the other hand on the mane of the unsaddled horse, Ridgway rode bravely. Somewhere along in my daydream, a man's sharp voice would jolt me back to reality.

"Sam! What are you doing, boy?" my father scolded. In spite of his tone, I recognized the strong current of affection that ran through his voice. On this occasion he quickly got my attention. "Sam, you better get a move on. The vet will be here in less than an hour, and if you don't get these sheep to pasture, you can't watch the operation."

"The operation!" That jerked me fully into reality. I took off at a trot with the goat right behind me. The foremost sheep trailed Old Goat, and after a minute or two even the sheep at the rear of the flock were moving. I was always a little slow on Saturdays in the fall, after watching the Devine High School football game the night before. But news of the veterinarian's imminent arrival perked me up, and I ran back the mile and a half to our barnyard, where the operation on our Duroc boar was to take place.

It was not easy to raise hogs in Texas in 1948, but it was not exceedingly difficult either. My dad often had said that the hogs were the most profitable animals on the farm. With their sale we could always pay for the feed to winter over the cattle and horses. A sow would give birth to eight or ten pigs, then, only six months later, produce a new litter. This capability ensured a constant supply of new pigs; they grew fast, reaching market size in half a year.

The present boar had reigned for more than a generation of swine, and the laws of genetics, as interpreted by our agriculture teacher, Mr. Henry Moss, dictated that a new sire was in order. But the old boar would not be wasted because we would butcher him for ham and bacon. To prepare him for his fate, the old boar had to be castrated. Boar meat was tough and foul-smelling, but if the animal were castrated and fed properly for a time, the meat would become more tender, and the disagreeable odor would subside.

Puffing and out of breath, I approached the barnyard. I heard the clang, clap, clang of the metal self-feeder lids opening and closing as I came to the fence along the feeder pen. The noise intensified as many pigs came over to the fence to greet me and perhaps, I imagined, to make inquiries about my trip or curry favor in hopes of winning their father's job.

The boar was in a small pen on the opposite side of the barn. Dad had arranged for several strong men to be there so they could hold the five-hundred-pound hog while the veterinarian worked. Dad and most of the other farmers did their own pig castrating, but since this was a special hog, bigger and stronger than most, they wanted to see how the vet would manage it.

Dr. Woodrow Sharp, the veterinarian from nearby Castroville, arrived and pulled on his clean rubber boots and a white coat. Handing me a shiny bucket, he asked me to fill it with clean water. When we arrived at the hog's pen, Dr. Sharp took a bottle of blue liquid from his bag and poured a hefty portion into the bucket I held. This drew a murmur of speculation from the assembled hog-holders now perched on a fence overlooking the boar. Dad explained to Dr. Sharp that he had plenty of manpower to help catch the hog and had assembled rope and various implements for restraining the animal. Dr. Sharp said he appreciated that very much. He would let Dad know when he needed help.

The doctor pulled a small piece of rope from his bag, made a loop in the end, and dangled this near the hog's nose. The swine chomped down. The loop wound up around the boar's snout, just behind the largest upper teeth. With the other end of the rope, Dr. Sharp deftly threw a half hitch and then a clove hitch around a post at the pen's corner. I recognized the knots immediately because I had just passed my second-class Boy Scout test. While the hog was engaged in a stubborn tug-o'-war with the post, Dr. Sharp went around to its other side and slipped another little white rope on one rear leg and a third on the other. He tethered the lines to the opposite fence.

In this manner, without so much as rumpling his coat, Dr. Sharp had the hog immobile. He stepped into the pen and began to spread a large cloth on the ground under the hog. He appeared more like a fastidious person preparing for a picnic than someone about to remove the private parts of a hog.

Dr. Sharp asked me to come into the pen and bring the bucket that now was filled with a deep blue fluid. He gave the hog a couple of injections and scrubbed the animal's hind parts with the blue liquid, then dried the area with a towel. I had never seen such cleanliness practiced around hogs.

Dr. Sharp removed two shiny instruments from his case. I looked up toward the pig's head, perhaps to observe him one last time in his whole state. The boar grunted. Then, hearing two dull thuds only a second or two apart, I looked down to see two pounds of glistening hog testicles lying on Dr. Sharp's picnic cloth. In a little more than a turn of the head, I had missed most of the operation. Now Dr. Sharp was putting in a suture. The released hog clambered into a trough to swill up a favorite bran and milk mixture that Dad had prepared. He didn't seem to notice anything amiss.

Carrying Dr. Sharp's bucket back to his car, I glowed with pride—all those grown men around, and I, a twelve-year-old kid, was the only one who got to help. The doctor was telling Dad how wise he had been for being so well prepared for the operation. When the vet was gone, Dad said to me, "Son, that's what you should be when you grow up, a vet like Dr. Sharp."

I readily agreed. I could not wait to tell all my friends at school. To my dismay, however, the teacher would not allow me to present my story of the hog castration in class the following Monday. "In town you just don't talk about that sort of thing in front of girls," counseled my friend John Watson at recess.

In spite of the social frustrations the profession seemed to promise, I knew I wanted to be a veterinarian and never considered another profession. Although I was unaware of it, other influences in my country life also were preparing me for my future. My first interest in something related to scientific research was, oddly enough, botanical. A major percentage of my waking hours between the ages of twelve and sixteen seemed to be consumed in a search for some local leaf or plant fiber that would make good smoking material. In those days the thought of marijuana never occurred to me. Even though in school we often sang a song in Spanish called "La Cucaracha," I was blissfully innocent of the content:

> La cucaracha, la cucaracha,
> ya no puede caminar,
> porque no tiene, porque le falta
> marijuana que fumar.

Marijuana was not in the picture, but what did attract me was chewing tobacco, because the users made it seem so appealing. Most of my early heroes chewed Brown Mule or Day's Work, which they stored in the hip pockets of their jeans or blue overalls. The large lump of tobacco in a man's jaw provided pleasure for hours as the chewer dug post holes, branded calves, baled hay, or rode broncs. Or so it seemed to me.

I was forbidden to purchase chewing tobacco, which was a problem of little concern to me, since I never had money anyway. So I experimented with readily available leaves and stems from the fields and pastures around my home. I dried my weeds, soaked them, marinated them in various concoctions, then chewed them or smoked them in brown paper "cigarettes." I tested virtually every leaf or plant that grew in our area, except those that I knew to be poisonous. In this way I came to admire scientific inquiry.

Such interests spurred me sufficiently to ensure reasonable attention to high school and eventual entry into college. (Obviously, I should not underestimate the influence of my parents, who encouraged me in other pursuits far less questionable than daydreaming or tobacco experimentation.) In the late summer of 1954, my dad deposited me at Texas A&M in College Station, Texas, in front of the Memorial Student Center, a tribute to the school's training of thousands of officers and men who had fought and died in the nation's wars.

My pilgrimage to veterinary science seemed, at the time, unnecessarily tedious. Suddenly my days were filled with chemistry and biology, microscopes, test tubes, and pickled frogs. Moreover, since Texas A&M was a military school, I also had to learn to march, salute, shine shoes, and make up a small bed daily. None of these skills has been of much benefit to me in the years since, though many swear by the strength of moral character these activities instilled in them. As for me, I was pleased that my obligation to the military tradition of Texas A&M was completed after two years. I moved to a room where neither the beds nor floors were inspected, where one could wear rough-out boots or U.S. Keds and walk naturally—out of step.

During my years in veterinary school I earned money by working for a scientist who was studying the mesquite, a small, often despised thorny tree that grows over much of the Southwest. My job was to remove the mesquite seeds from their pods, make a small hole in each one, then plant the seeds in flowerpots. At times two large greenhouses full of these pots with small growing trees were under my care. I watered them and measured them. Different poisons in various concentrations were applied to various groupings of these hardy plants. I don't know how it all turned out, but the last time I was in South Texas there seemed to be no shortage of mesquite.

At Texas A&M, I earned a bachelor's degree and then, in 1960, a degree of doctor of veterinary medicine. I was twenty-four years old, and after taking the state board examination, I was ready to go into practice, except for one technicality: I was eligible to be drafted. Aside from a troubling tendency to gain weight and an acquired cigar habit, I was physically healthy. No one looking at my 6-foot 2-inch, 250-pound frame would have suspected physical weakness. Nor did I have any pressing financial or family responsibilities. I had only just met my wife-to-be, a young Baylor University graduate, Jeanette Fuller, who was my brother Sid's high school English teacher. In a few months I would convince Jeanette to marry me, but at this time I was still single and couldn't think of any excuse to keep me away from the military draft. A certain caution about the possibility of being drafted into the army led me to apply for an air force commission, and in time the air force sent me to Oxnard Air Force Base.

In December 1960 Jeanette and I drove over the high rise of Conejo Grade in southern California. We had been traveling in warm weather in an open car. As we arrived at the top of the mountain road overlooking Pleasant Valley, a beautiful green plain planted with citrus groves and farms, we both exclaimed in delight at the sudden coolness of the Pacific breezes.

Marty braked suddenly. I awoke from my daydream as the pickup stopped before the service entrance at Pacific Ocean Park. When we arrived at the large pool, we were surprised to see that it was empty. Then we saw that all the dolphins were swimming in the shallow water of the inset small pool. Wally and Mo, dressed in their customary dolphin-catching attire—Mo in a diver's wet suit and Wally in his rubber overalls— were taking advantage of the lowered water level to clean the walls of the big tank. Mo waded in the shallow water, wielding a stiff, long-handled brush as he scrubbed algae from the tank sides. Meanwhile, Wally trudged back and forth with a large mop in his hands, jabbing and plunging under the surface.

As we came closer, I could see that Wally was standing guard while Mo worked. In his rubber suit, Wally appeared to be a strange knight with a padded, frayed jousting pole. His opponent, the scarred male Tuf Guy, now attacked and bit anyone or anything that entered the water. Whenever Tuf Guy charged at Mo, Wally would push the dolphin away with the spongy strands of the mop. As our group approached, the aggressor turned in the turbid green water to watch us for a moment. Then with renewed vigor he attacked Wally's mop, like a pup trying to wrest a favorite rag toy from its master's hand. But this "pup" weighed more than two hundred pounds, had almost one hundred sharp teeth, and, as Wally assumed based on recent experience, meant to play rough.

Wally continued to occupy Tuf Guy while Bill Scronce, Marty, and Mo caught Dash and put him in a sling. The overhead crane lifted Dash from the deep pool to the concrete platform where our truck was parked. As the sling passed by him, Wally slowly retreated, backing past the other dolphins. He drew a leg out of the pool and cautiously eased his body onto the dry concrete ledge, continuing to fend off Tuf Guy until he was a full mop- and arm-length away from the pool's edge. This procedure seemed a bit overcautious to me, but then the dolphin slid onto the concrete, furiously snapping his jaws and nodding his head. Only when Wally retreated about twenty feet and turned his back to grasp the topside ladder did the dolphin slide back into the pool. Witnessing these events, I was glad we had chosen Dash over Tuf Guy.

In contrast, our dolphin Dash seemed placid as we placed him on the rubber pad. When we brought the dolphin to Point Mugu, sailors and workmen who had been completing our facility crowded around the small truck to see the dolphin.

"Will dolphins bite?" one man asked.

"Yes," I quickly replied. "This one hasn't bitten anyone yet, but one that was with him down at POP certainly has. They have a hundred sharp teeth."

"Are they intelligent?" asked another sailor.

"Well, maybe," I replied. "That's one thing we plan to find out.

We put Dash into clean Pacific seawater, alone in a pool fifty feet in diameter and eight feet deep. We worried that he might suffer from loneliness, but the dolphin seemed to thrive, and Bob Bailey began to train him for experiments the NOTS scientists wanted to conduct. Plans were afoot to obtain more of the small whales from a source in Florida, so Dash would not be alone much longer. But I might have worried had I known that one of his companions was to be the feisty dolphin at POP that Wally had named Tuf Guy.

In the late spring of 1963 the dolphin research program at Point Mugu seemed to be asleep. As I was soon to discover, however, a chain of important events was about to get things moving. Three new dolphins arrived from Florida, followed shortly afterward by dolphin expert F.G. Wood, who left his position as curator of Florida Marineland to supervise our dolphin facility. Later I hired a lab assistant named Debbie Duffield, who became a great success as a dolphin trainer, and most important for the success of our project, we purchased the ailing dolphin Tuf Guy from the closing sea circus at Pacific Ocean Park.

The first link in this chain of acquisitions began when Dr. Lee Hall's secretary telephoned a message. "Be in Dr. Maag's office at three o'clock," she said. Dr. Clint Maag was the department head.

"Look, Sam," Clint said, handing me a document entitled *Dolphin Research Proposal*. "I've been thinking. Those guys from NOTS who wrote this proposal are coming down here planning to work with *Tursiops*

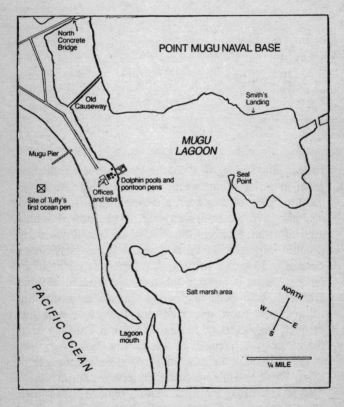

Point Mugu in 1964

Albert Einstein *truncatus*. I'm a psychologist, and you're a vet. Neither of us is a dolphin expert. But we both know that they will be lucky if these things are as trainable as dogs or pigs."

"You might be right," I agreed.

"Neither you nor I can tell the NOTS scientists when they are wrong," Clint continued. "To keep their feet on the ground, and to run a practical dolphin research facility, we need another person, someone with a great deal of cetacean experience." (We all knew by then that whales, dolphins, and porpoises were members of the biological order Cetacea. The official name for our facility, the concrete tank where Dash resided, was the Cetacean Research Facility, even though everyone at Point Mugu called it the porpoise pool.) "We want someone with management ability, someone with stature in the field, someone the NOTS scientists will listen to. The Office of Naval Research in Washington says that F.G. Wood of the original Marineland in Florida is the person for the job."

Clearly, Clint had been doing more than thinking about this. A few days later he appeared at our pool accompanied by Forrest Glenn Wood, Jr. "Call me Woody," Forrest said.

We didn't have much to show a visiting dolphin expert. Dash swam around, looking insignificant in the large concrete tank. "What do you think of him?" I asked, gesturing toward Dash, who eyed us suspiciously from the center of the tank.

"Well, he's a nice little porpoise. Looks healthy enough, at least as far as I can tell from here," replied Woody.

"You said 'porpoise,' Woody," Clint interrupted.

"Just what is the difference between a porpoise and a dolphin?"

Woody deliberated for an instant, then perhaps unconsciously he took on an authoritative posture, stepping forward slightly and drawing himself up to full height. *"Tursiops truncatus* is the scientific name," he began. "That we all agree upon. Porpoise and dolphin are common names, and neither has any scientific status nor generally agreed upon definition. There are about fifty species of small, toothed whales, from seas virtually the world over and a few river systems as well, that we call porpoises or dolphins. Some scientists make a distinction, calling the harbor porpoise and its close relatives by the name 'porpoise' and using the term 'dolphin' for others."

Woody paused, as if to emphasize what he was about to say. "I generally prefer the word 'porpoise.' A number of highly respected American cetologists follow long established usage and call all of the small toothed whales porpoises. This practice, if nothing else, avoids confusing the dolphin-mammal with the dolphin-fish."

A little intimidated by Woody's professional manner and command of precise detail, I uneasily ventured, "I guess it doesn't make much difference then whether we call them dolphins or porpoises if people understand that we are talking not about fish but about warm-blooded, air-breathing mammals like ourselves."

Woody's steady gaze halted me. "I have found that the distinction is more easily made by most people in this country if I call them porpoises," he said evenly.

Two months later, Bill Scronce, Marty, and I visited Florida Marineland, where Woody was curator, to pick up three new dolphins. Near here one can drive over a bridge and often see dolphins swimming from the sea into the fresh water of St. John's River. The first permanent colony of captive dolphins was begun in Marineland's large tanks in 1938. Much of what was known about dolphins up to the sixties had come from this place that many aptly called a "window on the sea." For example, dolphin sonar was discovered in the murky waters of creeks and inlets near here. Arthur McBride, Woody's predecessor at Marineland, observed that dolphins managed to avoid a small-mesh net like that used for catching mullet and other small fish. Consequently, a large mesh of about ten inches had to be used to catch dolphins. Even in turbid water or at night when there was no possibility that the animals could see, the dolphins immediately escaped if the net's floating corkline was submerged. McBride suggested that the dolphins' behavior "calls to mind the sonic sending and receiving apparatus which enables the bat to avoid obstacles in the dark." Within a decade of McBride's original observations, William Schevill and Barbara Lawrence of Woods Hole Oceanographic Institution (in Massachusetts) and Winthrop Kellogg of Florida State University had demonstrated through careful experiments that dolphins did indeed have a superb sonar.

At Marineland I saw shows that demonstrated some of the impressive skills of dolphins. First I saw dolphins of all ages cavort in the main tank, playing catch with tourists as they hurled rubber balls or small inflatable inner tubes. In a similar game a man in a sailor suit wielded a sawed-off oar to bat a huge rubber baseball. The gray forms of smiling dolphins crowded together, standing high above the surface on tail flukes that furiously beat the water as they vied to catch the wet spinning sphere. The winner dolphin held the ball between its jaws for a moment, then with considerable strength and grace hurled it back to the man. Next I watched a dolphin basketball game at the stadium tank. A dolphin moved forward slowly, hitting the ball in a staccato rhythm with its snout; then, in a deft move at midtank, the dolphin passed by the ball and with powerful flukes kicked it high in the air. The animal then raced forward to poke the falling oval as it hit the water and took up the dribbling again for a short distance. Lifting the sphere with its rounded snout, the dolphin pitched the ball perfectly into the basket.

The rhythm and timing of the basketball-playing dolphin were nearly perfect. I marveled, not that the trick was done by the dolphin but that it was done so expertly. I asked Fred Lyons, the head trainer, how he had trained the tail kick in the middle of the dribbling. "She initiated that herself," he said. "Since it looked so good, we let her keep it."

During our visit to Florida, the Marineland collecting crew caught the three dolphins that were to be donated to our project in California. We went all the way across the continent to get dolphins, ignoring the thousands of white-sided and common dolphins just off Point Mugu because the hardy Atlantic bottlenosed dolphins were easier to keep in captivity. In the deep Pacific waters no one had yet been able to catch bottlenosed dolphins consistently. Fishermen in Florida, however, could catch dolphins in shallow bays, channels, inland waterways, and even creeks and rivers. These fishermen used large seines with which they could capture a whole group of animals at once.

We flew back to Point Mugu with the three new

dolphins, feeling that our trip to Marineland had been a success. We also were pleased to learn that Woody had accepted the offer to supervise our research team. A few weeks later the Marineland curator joined us in California. In the months that followed, as I continued my education on dolphins, Woody was an inspiring, if at times intimidating, teacher.

By summer's end I decided I knew enough about dolphins to start research of my own. I was particularly interested in dolphin medical care, but I also wanted to know how dolphins can hold their breath so long and dive so often without problems from the "bends," the decompression disorder that affects human divers who return to the surface too rapidly after a deep dive. Before such ambitious projects could be tackled, however, I had to solve basic problems such as determining a dolphin's normal levels of blood sugar, sodium, potassium, cholesterol, and bilirubin. Indeed, the list of things yet to be discovered about the physiology of dolphins seemed almost endless.

Over the winter I made great progress on my projects. At the time I was totally involved in the dolphin research at Point Mugu, and I heard nothing from Wally and Mo at Pacific Ocean Park. Then one day in March 1964 Bill Scronce brought me some disturbing news: Both Mo and Wally were out of a job. POP had sold the two large performing dolphins, Lana and Toro, but no one wanted to take Tuf Guy. The dolphin had been sick, and potential buyers didn't think he would live. "Mo wants us to bring Tuf Guy to Point Mugu. The price is one hundred fifty dollars," Bill told me.

As soon as possible I talked with Woody, who was

in charge of our funds. Since I had been asking to have my own experimental dolphin, Woody agreed to buy Tuf Guy. He moved the requisition through the supply department in record time, and by midafternoon that day, the dolphin was in our care at Point Mugu.

Tuf Guy was emaciated. The dolphin had lost so much weight that the transverse spines of vertebrae appeared as bumps protruding in a row on either side of his body from shoulder to tail fluke. He shivered as I examined his eyes and mouth, but he still had enough spunk to threaten me weakly with open jaws. Thirty-five pounds lighter, dispirited, and covered with tooth marks from the attacks of larger dolphins, this was a much different Tuf Guy than the one who had taken my thermometer eighteen months before. Bill and a couple of sailors easily held the animal while I took blood, gave injections, and treated scrapes, bites, and scratches on the dolphin's body.

When we put Tuf Guy into Tank 2, a plastic pool set up on the sand beside Mugu Lagoon, he swam counterclockwise in tight circles. I was relieved when he accepted a half-dozen mackerel, but he regurgitated two of them ten minutes later. Woody came out to the beach to see our new acquisition and remarked, "He's not a very healthy-looking dolphin. What's his name?"

"Tuf Guy," I replied. "That's what Wally named him soon after they brought him from Gulfport to POP."

"If your treatment works and he lives," said Woody, "why don't we shorten that name to Tuffy?"

Lab tests revealed that Tuffy had an infection and anemia. The next day the dolphin showed no improvement. He took a few fish, then threw up again and would eat nothing afterward. In the late afternoon Tuffy took a fish in his mouth, holding it crosswise so the tail trailed out one corner and the head out the other. The dolphin carried the fish for about ten minutes and then spat it out. "He acts as if he wants to eat but just doesn't dare," said one of my helpers.

Something about her comment clicked. Woody had mentioned that he had seen ulcers in dolphins in Florida. Dr. Robert Miller had found ulcers in Lags at POP. An ulcer might account for Tuffy's throwing up and his refusal to eat even though he appeared hungry.

That afternoon and again the following morning we drained the pool. I passed a stomach tube to pump in medication and injected Tuffy with more drugs. We planned to repeat this procedure twice each day until the animal's appetite improved. The next morning I packed fish with large white antacid tablets and asked a trainer who was working in an adjacent pool to try to get Tuffy to eat the fish during breaks in his session.

Our tests showed no improvement, but during the morning Tuffy ate all the medicated fish that I had left and several others as well. The trainer explained that when Tuffy took the first fish, he circled the tank very slowly, holding the fish in his mouth, as he had done before, then spit it out. In fifteen minutes, when the trainer checked Tuffy again, the fish was gone. He offered another. The dolphin took it but repeated the previous behavior—mouthing the fish, then spitting it out, and only eating when the trainer turned away again. In this manner Tuffy took a fish every ten or fifteen minutes during the morning.

That afternoon the sick dolphin ate nine pounds of fish, more than half the usual daily ration for a dolphin his size. The following day Tuffy ate thirteen pounds, and we shifted all the medication to types that could be given in the fish. Soon he was eating seventeen to twenty-two pounds of smelt and mackerel a day, about ten thousand calories or enough daily nutrition for three two-hundred-pound steelworkers. In another week the knobby protrusion of vertebrae on the sides of the body began to disappear, the hollow beside the dorsal fin filled in, and the indentation behind the head became less prominent.

Although Tuffy gained weight, he remained unfriendly. He would come to the side of the pool to take a fish but would not allow the feeder to touch him. When he was not hungry, the dolphin kept his distance, eyeing people suspiciously from the center of the pool.

Because Tuffy's pool needed repairs, we had to move him to the main concrete pool. I planned to take advantage of the move by treating Tuffy's cuts and taking a blood sample. (I had learned to draw blood from the tail flukes, where blood vessels run near the surface like the veins of a maple leaf.) We drained the pool just after seven o'clock inspection, when a crew of sailors was available to help catch and hold the dolphin. This morning Tuffy was not easy to catch or to hold. Although return of his pugnacious temperament signaled improved health, I was sorry to see I hadn't cured the dolphin's bad temper along with his ulcers, anemia, and infection.

Once Tuffy was caught, the four largest sailors helped Marty and Bill Scronce hold him while I treated the numerous raking tooth marks that probably were inflicted by the dolphin Toro during the last days in the tank at POP. I cleaned the tail flukes with alcohol and prepared to put a tiny needle in the central blood vessel.

This vessel is part of the dolphin's unique adaptation to its ocean environment. In land mammals, including humans, arteries that run out to the appendages are accompanied by large veins that return the circulated blood to the heart. Dolphins and whales, however, have a complex of small veins surrounding the artery. This arrangement helps the animal to keep warm in cold water and to cool down from the heat of exertion.

If the dolphin is quiescent, the blood pumped out to the flukes, flippers, and dorsal fin flows back to the heart through veins surrounding the artery, keeping the warmth from the blood deep inside. On exertion the dolphin's blood pressure and temperature rise and the artery bulges, making less space for the surrounding veins and forcing some blood to return to the heart by a system of veins near the surface. These surface veins dump more body heat to the sea. Thus the dolphin is able to shed its "overcoat" of blubber temporarily.

As I inserted the sharp needle, Tuffy's anger welled up and he screeched raspingly. Bending over the fluke, straining to see the faint line marking the blood vessel, I put myself in jeopardy of a broken nose should Tuffy free himself from the blanket of human flesh that held him to a soggy foam-rubber mat. Now the dolphin's anger worked to the benefit of all concerned. The artery bulged, and bright red blood flowed into my syringe. I had my sample in thirty seconds.

The large concrete pool, scrubbed and filled with clean seawater, was ready for Tuffy. At my signal the sailors dropped one side of the sling and let Tuffy plop into the clear water. The skinny animal circled the pool slowly at its perimeter, right against the wall. When first introduced to a pool, the dolphins generally stayed near the center and swam in small circles, avoiding the walls and objects or people near the edge. But Tuffy swam around the pool's edge first at the surface, then at mid-depth, with his head scanning from left to right, his body cocked to one side, as if examining the barrier. Pausing for a pair of breaths and to peer briefly back at us, he dove to the bottom and circled the perimeter again, as if to check the seam between the tank's walls and bottom. The dolphin made two of these slow circuits around the bottom perimeter before pausing at the slatted, wooden spillway gate over which water from the pool flowed through a concrete flume into Mugu Lagoon.

Facing the wooden spillway, the dolphin went up and down the obstacle, poking his snout at every crevice, turning upside down to examine the wood from every angle. We listened to his buzzing sonar sounds through the hydrophone amplifier that hung outside the sound-recording trailer adjacent to the pool. His intense inspection took about fifteen minutes; then Tuffy seemed satisfied with his new surroundings and resumed swimming in his ordinary way.

Near midnight that same day I came in to try to feed Tuffy the medicine he needed every six hours. On this foggy night a single light shone over one edge of the pool. My world above the pool was a gray envelope surrounded by darkness. I could barely see through the fog to the far edge of the still pool.

Creeping around the perimeter in my rubber shoes, I found Tuffy lying on the surface with his head propped on the gate, where three inches of water spilled into the flume. Both his eyes were closed. Concerned, I sat quietly and timed his breathing. Twice each minute the dolphin's flukes swept slightly downward, his blowhole opened, and his chest compressed then expanded as the lungs exchanged air.

Did Tuffy know the way out, I wondered? Perhaps he just wanted to be here in case the dam broke. At high tide he could jump the gate, swim through the flume into the lagoon, then head through its mouth to the open sea. I could not prevent it.

I left the sleeping dolphin to get some fish for the medication. When the first fish hit the water, Tuffy started. A wave of motion sped along his body, his head lifted, his flukes moved down, and he was off like a shot. Light shining through the clear pool reflected from the white walls so I could see every detail under the surface. As the dolphin swam, tiny fish scales, beach sand, or diatoms spun away, creating little tinsel showers in the dolphin's wake. He slowed and coasted toward the center of the pool to pick up the mackerel. Approaching the fish, Tuffy cocked so far over on his right side that he was almost upside down. He did not tarry near the bottom, nor did he carry the fish. He swallowed the food without pausing, came toward the edge, and waited at the surface about ten feet from me.

He swallowed the pill-laden fish I threw as soon as it hit the water. I shoveled in another twenty mackerel, one at a time. The fish seemed to slow only slightly as each slid headfirst down the dolphin's throat. They would be stew in twenty minutes, and in an hour they'd be reduced to a pile of white translucent bones in the inner compartment I called the forestomach. The stew would then continue on to the other stomach compartments and into the intestine to be absorbed.

Tuffy's health continued to improve, and the stronger he grew, the more difficult to handle he became. The experienced trainers, old hands like Bill and Marty, now found themselves busy with other dolphins when word got around that I was collecting a crew to catch Tuffy. I had to rely on other helpers. The sailors who were assigned to us for this work were of two types: intelligent young men, often college-educated, who volunteered for duty with us because of personal interest; and not-so-intellectual misfits who were awaiting discharge or disciplinary action. Because both types worked well around the dolphins, it was only through listening to their conversation that one could reliably tell them apart. One of the so-called misfits was called Growth. During succeeding examinations, things would have been very difficult if it hadn't been for Growth.

I don't know whether Growth was a first name, last name, some mispronounced approximation of a real name, or just a nickname that his mates gave, but Growth is all that he was ever called in my presence. He kept his hair neatly combed, seldom wore a shirt over his tanned, muscular torso, and never spoke. He obeyed orders promptly but in a slow, deliberate way. He seemed not to mind anything the other sailors did unless it mussed his hair. In that event he would take prompt, violent action. It happened infrequently—news traveled. Nevertheless, this tough sailor was gentle with our dolphins. As he held Tuffy's flukes while I took blood, things remained under control on our end. Granted, those who held the head often did not fare so well.

After drawing blood during an examination, I had to insert a catheter into the dolphin's bladder to take a urine sample. The urine-taking seemed to please Tuffy even less than the bleeding, so the sailors groaned in protest at this part of the examination. They had all been bruised at one time or another by Tuffy's snout or scraped by his teeth.

"Doc, just *show* him the catheter," suggested Gates, one of our more intellectual sailors. "The last time, you were on this end of the animal, and he urinated when you brought it out of the case. Maybe he'll do it again."

Anything was worth a try. Halfheartedly, I waved the thin rubber tube just in front of the dolphin's eye. The bright yellow liquid began to flow, and we caught the specimen in a large test tube. "He's mean, but he's getting smart," another sailor said.

Tuffy *was* proving to be smart, but we weren't making much progress training him because Bob Bailey and the other trainers were simply too busy with their own dolphins to spend time with Tuffy. Besides, Tuffy had done his best to discourage trainers. He had chased people from his pool and bashed shins with his snout. He was not reluctant to bite the hand that fed him.

I knew that we must tame this feisty dolphin. His cooperation was essential for the experiments we planned, since it would be necessary to handle the dolphin even more often. Eventually, we wanted Tuffy to wear a harness to which monitoring gear could be attached. I hoped we could tame Tuffy to accept the harness in the manner of a trained horse or guide dog, without first being caught or restrained.

While the experienced trainers hesitated to work with Tuffy, one person begged for the job. I had hired a biology student named Debbie Duffield as a research assistant. Now I worried that her laboratory tests, so important to my work, would be neglected if she took on the dolphin's training.

"But Doctor Sam," she said, being formal (usually it was just plain Sam), "I'll get the lab work done, I promise you. I'll work with Tuffy early in the morning and late in the afternoon and on weekends. Let me try it for a month. If the lab work isn't getting done, we can change back."

I agreed to let her try. We moved Tuffy from the large main pool back to a round plastic pool on the sand. The main pool was needed for other work; besides, the smaller pool could be drained more quickly when we had to catch Tuffy for experiments. The pool was near two others where more experienced trainers worked with Dash and a dolphin named Salty. Debbie wouldn't have to go far to ask advice.

That afternoon Debbie fed the dolphin about forty mackerel and more than one hundred smelt one at a time, trying to give meaning with each fish. At first she simply held a fish in the water and let Tuffy take it from her hand. Then she tried to touch the animal with her free hand each time he took a fish. By day's end she could touch the dolphin on the snout or lower jaw.

The water in the pool felt like ice water to bare skin, so before swimming with Tuffy, Debbie borrowed a wet suit from a sailor. The rubber suit fit tightly in some places and much too loosely in others, but it enabled her to stay in the water with Tuffy for two hours. When Debbie first entered the waist-deep water, Bill and I stood guard outside, ready for a rescue. Tuffy swam around the perimeter, creating a wave that rocked the walls of the small pool. But

Tuffy had more hunger than temper. He took a fish from Debbie's hand; then, as he paused for her next offering, he allowed her to touch his forehead. With each fish Debbie tried to increase the amount of time the dolphin remained near her and tolerated her touch. In the afternoon she held Tuffy briefly with one hand under his jaw while touching his dorsal fin with her other hand. "He seemed almost friendly today," Debbie reported.

The next day she continued the taming work and started to teach Tuffy retrieving. In three weeks she could pet the dolphin in the water and he would retrieve a ring or a float from any location in the pool. Debbie wrote the following in the codelike style that many of the trainers cultivated:

EUREKA!! A.M. Fed 11 lb.—worked well—spent most of my time working with his staying still while being touched. Retrieved well & instantly. Stayed still longer and didn't seem as touchy.

P.M. Worked 99% of time on remaining stationary. Did pretty well—started slipping hand around side towards flipper—good. Retrieved a few times. THEN: Removed fish pail from pool and stood by side for awhile. He came up and let me scratch under jaw and over melon [the dolphin's bulbous forehead]. Repeated—came back to be rubbed— getting no fish. Gradually let me rub middle of back—spent well over 20 minutes doing this—he came up with no hesitation and stayed for longer and longer.

Another big advance came about two weeks later. Tuffy appeared to enjoy being stroked and petted, but he seemed sensitive about where Debbie touched him.

One day, when she rubbed the dolphin in such a way that a zipper on her wet suit got caught behind Tuffy's flipper, the dolphin whirled instantly and bit her hand. The dolphin's sharp teeth left eleven round punctures in Debbie's palm and wrist. Blood dripped from the holes and washed off in the cold seawater. Yet in spite of the painful wound, Debbie stayed in the pool and continued to stroke the animal.

"It was strange," said Debbie. "After that bite Tuffy seemed to trust me completely. I could touch him anywhere, I could rub him, and I could pull on any part of his body. He became more willing to work."

I was elated by Debbie's accomplishments, and almost everyone at the facility was visibly impressed. Still, one never knew what Tuffy would do next, and I knew we had a long way to go before approaching our ultimate goal of working with the dolphin in the open ocean.

5

I was responsible for the well-being of all the navy's dolphins at Point Mugu, not just Tuffy. Consequently, I sometimes had to leave my research dolphin to tend to others. On one occasion, for example, I flew to Gulfport, Mississippi, to look after a pair of newly captured navy dolphins during their air transport to Animal Behavior Enterprises in Hot Springs, Arkansas, where they would be trained. Some of the things I learned on this trip applied to my later work with Tuffy.

Like Tuffy, these dolphins were caught in the shallow waters of the Mississippi Sound by shrimp fishermen who were knowledgeable in the ways of bottle-nosed dolphins. From the capture location, we drove to the air base near Gulfport in a flatbed truck carrying two boxes, each containing a dolphin resting on its side covered by a moist sheet. During the drive the dolphins seemed to converse. One dolphin whistled, and the other answered. Sometimes both called in rapid succession. As we sped along, my white lab coat flapping in the wind, I struggled to hold my balance on the bed of the truck while I moved between the boxes, using the sprayer to moisten the dolphins. The dark eyes of the dolphins followed my movements.

Passers-by must have wondered why a man in a full-length lab coat with a stethoscope in the side pocket was lurching around two coffinlike boxes on a flatbed truck with a garden sprayer in his hands. At one red light a red convertible with the top down pulled alongside, and a young boy wearing a baseball cap and chewing a candy stick stood in the back seat. He yelled, "Hey, what do you have in the boxes, mister?" I didn't answer. "What are you spraying, mister?" he persisted.

Just then, the young male dolphin arched his body, managing to peer over the edge of his box for an instant. "Dad, Dad," the boy shouted, pounding his father on the shoulder and pointing. "A big fish, a big fish, it looked at us!" The father looked at me suspiciously, then reached back and pulled his boy into the front passenger seat.

We arrived at the airport without further incident. Soon two gray dolphins reclined in a navy airplane. After we were airborne, the commander left his co-pilot in charge of the flight deck and came back to check his unusual cargo. He watched for a moment as we went to and fro spraying gray skin, taking temperature and heartbeat measurements, and recording data in a notebook. "What do you tranquilize them with?" the pilot asked.

I explained that attempts to anesthetize dolphins had all ended in the animals' deaths. "The dolphin's respiration is so sensitive that we were afraid even to use tranquilizers. No medication was used to calm them," I said.

Despite their exterior calm, the dolphins' metabolism was generating heat. After an hour the skin on the underside was ninety degrees, the upper side was seventy, and the rectal temperature was ninety-eight. Every hour three of us would line up alongside each of the dolphins, remove all wristwatches and rings that could injure the animal's sensitive skin, and turn the animal onto the opposite side. Next we used a vacuum hose to suck excrement from the boxes to the exterior of the plane, spreading a fine mist of dolphin dung through the clouds over northern Mississippi and southern Arkansas.

Reporters with cameras met the plane at the air base in Little Rock. It was not generally appreciated, even in Arkansas, that the best place for advanced animal training was a farm in the rolling country just outside the city of Hot Springs. This farm was headquarters of Animal Behavior Enterprises (ABE), a private company that for about ten years had been selling trained animal acts and consulting with other organizations about animal training. ABE had come to be respected as a leader in the field.

Eventually, our two new dolphins would have to swim at full speed in the open ocean for Dr. Tom Lang's hydrodynamics tests, designed to help navy engineers build torpedoes and submarines that could glide through the water as efficiently as a dolphin. A major question was whether a dolphin could be released in the open sea and then enticed back to its trainers. To speed these tests along, Dr. Lang had arranged for the dolphins and their trainers to be coached by the ABE staff.

Some of the ABE people were well known to me. Kent Burgess, one of our teachers in the days of "chicken dance school" back at Point Mugu, was in charge of the daily instruction of our trainers and dolphins. Mr. and Mrs. Keller Breland, founders of ABE, were advisors to the Marinelands in Florida and California and to our research program. The Brelands had a simple, no-nonsense approach and a history of success in animal training that impressed the navy managers. I got to know Keller Breland and also found him impressive on a personal level.

I guessed that Keller was about fifty years old. His penetrating gaze could intimidate, but his eyes also could light up with cheer. As he told his tales, he blinked over a rounded belly from behind a fat cigar. I liked him from the start.

"Come on in the house," he said, after the dolphins were safely in their pools. "Let's have a little prayer meeting." The subject of this "prayer meeting," a long discussion of the matters that interested us, finally got around to the one that most occupied us: how to train captive dolphins so they could be set free in the open ocean to work under our control. There was little agreement among researchers that this so-called "open ocean control" of a dolphin could be achieved.

Keller had developed animal psychology into an engineering discipline at ABE. He had worked with forty species and more than four thousand individual animals. He was opposed to punishment in animal training and relied almost completely on reward. Thus the animal's hunger drive was important to his approach. This seemed to suggest that Keller's behavioral engineering could be successful only if we had complete control of the dolphin's food. In a meeting back at Point Mugu the consensus on this point had been expressed by Dr. Tom Milburn, the senior psychologist: "I cannot imagine using cut fish as a method of controlling the behavior of the dolphin when the latter is in the open sea and has free access to fish, as well as access to the companionship of its fellows." Nevertheless, Keller and Dr. Lang had convinced the navy it was worth a try.

We discussed and debated details of the proposed experiments, but we also lapsed into speculation about the many other things we could do with trained dolphins in the open sea: test their deep diving, train them to find specific objects in the sea, or train them to protect human divers from sharks. Secretly, I hoped I might train Tuffy for such tasks.

The following morning Bob Bailey and Bill Scronce began to work with the dolphins. Since my job of seeing that the animals arrived at ABE in good health and making sure the facilities were adequate for their three-month stay was completed, I prepared to return to Point Mugu. On my last day in Arkansas Keller agreed to give me a tour of ABE, whose main business was to provide trained animals for displays and amusement parks, for filmed commercials, and for various shows put on by animal trainers. Some of the trained animals worked in cages connected to coin-operated machines. A coin in the slot got a chicken to dance, a duck to beat a drum, or a rabbit to run out and nuzzle a plastic female bunny in a long dress.

"You always learn the most from your failures," Keller advised. He went on to tell of his "$8,000 Rump Roast Failure," about a cow trained to act in a skit that did not work out; "The Hoarding Hamster

Failure," about hamsters that would stop responding when their cheek pouches were filled; and the "Larcenous Turkey Failure," about a turkey, trained to deposit coins in a piggy bank, that began to swallow the coins.

"This is an important behavior for you to watch out for with your porpoises," explained Keller. "The turkey learned to pick up the coins just fine. It would deposit the coins in the bank, then the feeder would drop out grain for the turkey to eat. That all went according to plan. But picking up the coin became associated with the sound of the feeder dispensing food, and this sound with the eating of grain. Consequently, the turkey soon was swallowing the coins.

"The best porpoise at St. Augustine died because of this object-food relationship," Keller continued. "Of course, at the time we had no notion that this could happen. We trained the porpoise to fetch a rubber baseball. Upon returning the baseball to the trainer, the animal got a fish. Sure enough, one day the porpoise came back to the trainer with no ball in sight. They searched the bottom of the pool and all around. Finally they realized that the ball was in the animal's stomach. During attempts to remove the ball, the porpoise went into shock and died. The remedy, as you may have seen, was to use a ball so large that a porpoise cannot possibly swallow it.

"You know," he said, "another problem is the porpoise's reputation. People have the perception that these animals are unusually intelligent, perhaps more so than humans. There is even talk about a dolphin language." He paused, puffing on his cigar. "They may be smart, but that doesn't necessarily make them easy to train."

"Yes, I know," I answered. "Some people at Point Mugu have been surprised that the dolphins don't immediately understand and do what is required. Some are disappointed that dolphin training seems to be the same slow process that it is with more familiar animals."

"The quickest way to train a porpoise," said Keller, "is by simple procedures that break down the desired behaviors into small steps. It is slow, but this method is the quickest way to communicate with any animal, whether it is a chicken, a rat, a chimp, or a porpoise."

As I listened to Keller during that tour, I learned that the Brelands had brought mass production to animal training. "I would have no hesitation," said Keller, "in signing a contract to teach a million chickens to dance. If you have the money, I can get a million hens doing the twist."

His manner was so relaxed and the methods he described so simple that anything seemed possible, yet I was not prepared for the assembly-line process we saw on entering the main barn of the Breland Farm. The barn was filled with machinery. Overhead a hen walked a tightrope. When the hen reached a pedestal at the end, a bell rang; she turned immediately to hurry down the rope to the opposite end, where she pecked up a yellow grain of corn and turned again to repeat the performance. On ground level other chickens clawed at the training cage floor in the beginnings of the chicken "dance" movements; ducks drummed and fluffy rabbits scurried out to buss white plastic bunnies that glowed pink for an instant, signaling Fluffy to turn tail and enter a small wooden house to collect its reward.

As I stood with Keller in the middle of this unique barn, I felt as if I had been transported to a surrealistic factory. Bells clanged, buzzers buzzed, wheels turned, belts moved, objects tumbled through chutes, and workers bustled about. Stacks of poultry crates stood near the doorway, some containing animals waiting their turn at the machines, others empty and waiting to carry graduate workers to circus jobs far away.

Overhead the hen moved back and forth on the tightrope, eyes straight ahead. These healthy animals seemed to show a mindless devotion to their simple tasks. I wondered, however, whether this powerful concentration was driven by fear of deviating from the method that satisfied hunger. In any case, each animal achieved a degree of precision that made it seem a part of the equipment, like wheels, wires, nuts, and rods.

Not altogether, though. I spied a rabbit with large brown spots moving quietly down the wall under the chicken tightrope-walker toward a darkened corner. Keller also saw the stray, for he began moving in that direction, picking his way between the machines. None of the apparatus missed a bell or a clang, nor did any of the working animals take the least notice as Keller grabbed the errant bunny. "It's probably an equipment failure," he said as we moved back across the barn. "We have a lot more trouble with the machines than with the animals."

Too bad, I thought to myself. I had hoped that somehow in this rabbit we had found an individual. But, alas, it was not so. A food pellet or something had gotten stuck in the gears. Keller quickly fixed the contraption, and the brown-and-white bunny was again set on track, scurrying back and forth, hugging plastic to collect food pellets.

If a stuck food hopper can cause a trained rabbit to

stray, I thought, what chance do we have of keeping a hungry dolphin from swimming away? On my way back to California, I pondered this question. Remembering Debbie's success with Tuffy during the weeks since she had started training the dolphin, I began to feel more confident. Someday, I believed, Tuffy would work for us while free in the open sea.

Our plans for Tuffy changed somewhat, but not for the worse, when the public affairs people decided to take advantage of the presence of film star Glenn Ford, who was a navy reserve commander doing active duty at Point Mugu. They hoped to have the famous actor narrate a film about our work with the dolphins, featuring Tuffy working blindfolded to demonstrate dolphin sonar.

Tuffy had been trained to retrieve a plastic float, a cork, a sailor's hat, or a rubber ring thrown into the pool. Now he would have to find the object wearing blinders. We also wanted to show that a blindfolded dolphin could navigate, and we hoped to have him swim through a series of hoops.

The training was easier than might have been expected because dolphins are nosy animals. They like to poke or root at things. Debbie had attached a lead-weighted wooden disk to a cloth ring; when she put it in the water, Tuffy poked it. Then Debbie blew her whistle and gave the animal a fish. By repeating this she was able to move the cloth ring onto his snout. When the ring was on Tuffy's snout, she began pushing the animal away. Tuffy then had to swim back toward Debbie so she could take the ring and give another fish. Soon, whenever the weighted ring was thrown into the pool, Tuffy would poke his snout through, fish the ring off the bottom, and carry the object back to Debbie.

By now Tuffy would poke his snout into almost anything thrown into the pool and return it. When Debbie threw in the hoop, Tuffy brought it back. With the animal accustomed to the hoop, she held it in the water in front of Tuffy, while dangling a fish on the opposite side. He poked his snout through to get the fish. Now she held the fish farther and farther out until the animal had to come through the hop to get it. At first Tuffy swam through one hoop whenever it was put into the water. A second hoop was put in, and he was required to go through both before the reward was given. Finally a third, then a fourth hoop were added.

It was necessary not only that Tuffy navigate through the series of hoops but also that he do it on signal. For this, Tuffy's behavior of swimming through the hoops whenever they were put into the water had to be extinguished. ("Extinguished" refers to the process whereby an animal quits performing a trained behavior that is not rewarded.) To signal Tuffy's hoop run, we found a small sounder that made a steady "beep, beep, beep" signal underwater. The device had a sea-water switch that actuated whenever Debbie put it in the water. Pulling the sounder out of the water stopped the current flow, and the device no longer sounded.

When Debbie put the hoops in the water, Tuffy went racing through. But this time there was no whistle and no reward. Tuffy treaded water on his tail, did a short jump, and made a rasping sound through his blowhole, then stayed open-mouthed in front of Debbie for thirty seconds. But no fish appeared. Debbie put in the beeper. Tuffy raced over and poked it. Debbie yanked the beeper out. Still no whistle and no fish. Debbie put the beeper in again. Again when the dolphin poked the beeper, out it came.

The dolphin appeared to know that Debbie wanted something different, but he seemed to be trying various actions randomly, trying to hit on something that would bring the whistle and reward. Debbie decided to put the beeper in the water just before the dolphin reached the first hoop on another run. After an hour Tuffy was going through the hoops when the beeper was put in the water. Now and then he still would make a run without the beeper, but since he didn't get rewarded for these runs, they became fewer and fewer.

One evening after Debbie had left the hoops in the pool, I found Tuffy swimming through the triad of hoops time after time, maybe practicing for tomorrow, perhaps just playing. In any case, the dolphin seemed to enjoy the sport. Another time, when Debbie took the morning off, she came in by the pool about noon. Walking by Tuffy, she suddenly heard the "beep, beep, beep" of the sounder for the hoop run. She feared that the beeper had fallen into the water and that Tuffy's well-established hoop-running skills might be extinguished. Debbie ran around the pool's edge, looking into the water. Tuffy followed eagerly after the trainer, who soon noticed that the beeping sound was following her too. One beep was off-key and sputtered slightly. Watching the crescent slit in Tuffy's head, she saw that the nasal plug that closed Tuffy's blowhole between breaths was moving just slightly with the beeps. Moving air through valves and sacs below the nasal plug with the skill of a trained musician, the dolphin duplicated the sound he yearned to hear. Debbie rushed to her cabinet to check out her theory; sure enough, the sounder was stored safely in its place. The hungry dolphin was generating his own beeps.

The next step was to train Tuffy to wear blinders. At the Florida Marineland, Woody had to train a dolphin to wear suction cup blinders because the dolphin's smooth, streamlined body was not easy to bandage, strap, or tie things to. We decided to employ Woody's technique with an improved suction cup made of safe materials. The cup had to stick to the animal's slick skin for at least ten minutes and be easy to put on and take off. We gave our specifications to the plastic materials engineer at Point Mugu, who came up with an opaque white silicone cup that seemed ideal. "I made a mold," he said, handing me a dozen of the cups. "The material isn't expensive. Let me know if you want more."

I rushed out to Tuffy's pool and handed Debbie one smooth white cup. When she put it in the water, the dolphin came over to poke it. After Tuffy had touched the cup, we decided to stick it to the side of his body. When the dolphin got used to the cup, we planned to move it gradually over the eye.

When Debbie attached the cup, Tuffy bolted. The dolphin shot around the tank as if trying to dislodge the leechlike suction cup clinging to his right flank. Whizzing around the pool to gain momentum, he jumped high in the air and crashed down hard on his right side where the cup was attached. Each time the dolphin came down, water splashed over the edges of the small plastic pool, rocking and swaying its walls. The cup slowly moved back on his body but did not shake loose. We stood by, helpless to intervene.

After a minute or so the dolphin's frenzy subsided,

and he settled into a stubborn pout. Tuffy swam slowly across the pool, arching his back, snapping his jaws, nodding, and making those familiar rasping sounds. The dolphin butted into the tank wall opposite Debbie and me and stayed there, head down, snout and forehead pressed against the wall, streams of bubbles coming from his blowhole.

We waited. Tuffy pouted, head pressed hard against the pool wall. The dolphin remained in this posture for almost three minutes; then we saw his body relax. He turned, looked toward us, and swam back, mouth open to take a fish, as if all were completely forgiven. Debbie removed the cup and rewarded the dolphin.

After this episode Debbie had little trouble getting Tuffy to accept the suction cup blinders. In three days he willingly wore them on both eyes. We noticed remarkably little difference in the dolphin's underwater behavior when the blinders were on. He could immediately retrieve objects from anywhere in the pool, avoid any obstacle, find a fish tossed anywhere, and unhesitantly return to the trainer.

I found it hard to imagine how sound traveling back and forth between the dolphin and his surroundings could carry so much information. Sound gave Tuffy an image that must have been almost as good as our visual image. Certainly, we concluded, he was a sonar operator par excellence. But dolphins use sound for more than sonar. Like other animals, dolphins employ sound for communication. People talk to one another, birds chirp in the trees, and wolves call to one another across the wilderness night. The varied types of sound produced by dolphins reminded us, in some ways, of the communication of each of these animals, yet we had no idea what the peculiar whistles, pulses, and numerous other dolphin sounds meant.

During that summer of 1964 it often seemed that we were getting nowhere with our dolphin research. In looking back, however, I realize it was then that real progress actually began. At the time Debbie and I were fully involved in the training of Tuffy, and we were rapidly accumulating data from our experiments in dolphin physiology.

Much of our time was taken up assisting the scientists who visited our facility, some for a day, some for a week, and others for a whole summer. They designed experiments that asked many interesting questions of the dolphins. Although some got answers, others found only more questions. Most worked quietly, completed their experiments, and published their results, advancing our knowledge another step. I learned something from each researcher, but some, frankly, were pains in the neck. Their expectations were too great, or they just were not prepared to work with dolphins. Frequently they got in the way of our own progress. Nevertheless, all these characters are memorable, and in some ways I learned the most from the most eccentric ones.

Because these visiting scientists blur together in my memory, I have constructed a fictional composite, whom I call "Dr. Veruccus." Of course, I have never known anyone actually bearing the Latin name for wart, but the analogy is apt. Some people can wish warts away, but I can't. After a long stay, about the time I become accustomed to them, mine just vanish; but I always remember that I had a wart there. It was the same with my visiting scientists.

Dr. Veruccus arrived from the Midwest near the middle of June. Veruccus was tall but not as tall as his slimness made him seem. Standing next to him, I judged that he was a little under six feet in thick-soled shoes. His feet were large and appeared even larger because his trousers ended just above prominently protruding ankle bones emerging from heavy plaid socks stuffed into scuffed loafers.

Dr. Veruccus, a psychologist, already had established himself in the animal behavior field. Perhaps I shouldn't admit it, but I grew tired of hearing it said that with his help our project would cease drifting and get down to basic science. I think Woody, our facility director, was the only one who reckoned how difficult the shift from white rats to dolphins would be for Veruccus, whose two objectives were to find out about dolphin intelligence with discrimination tests and to get some idea of how dolphins might communicate with humans. Woody was skeptical. Veruccus expected to accomplish entirely too much in one summer. Our director pointed out to the visiting scientist that most of the claims for dolphin intelligence were greatly inflated. "There is no scientific evidence to support that," I often heard Woody caution Veruccus.

"The psychophysical techniques that I use will collect the evidence rapidly," claimed Veruccus.

Veruccus's first experiment, a discrimination test, aimed to learn whether a dolphin could tell the difference between two geometric shapes. Two shapes were to be presented to the dolphin, which was to pick the designated shape—for example, the square. It would then be trained to pick the square when it was paired with a triangle, a circle, a rectangle, and so on. The speed with which an animal learns always to pick the square gives some idea of its relative intelligence, at least if we use the term "intelligence" loosely.

For this experiment Veruccus needed his own dolphin. He was in luck because two dolphins recently had arrived at Point Mugu fresh from their course at ABE in Arkansas, and Bob Bailey had decided to concentrate his efforts on them. Having given up on Dash as a prospect for open ocean research, Bob assigned him to Veruccus, who began training him for the experiment.

At the moment our own priority was to prepare Tuffy for the film to be narrated by Glenn Ford. After that project I wanted the dolphin to help answer some of my questions about diving physiology. For example, how long could a dolphin comfortably hold its breath? My assistant had found a simple way to get the answer from Tuffy. Debbie noticed that when she stroked Tuffy's white underbelly, he happily remained quite still on his back at the surface for a minute or two. Of course, in this position the dolphin's blowhole is immersed; consequently, the animal cannot breathe. As Debbie stroked the dolphin, she could hold her hand on his chest and feel his heartbeat to time his pulse.

Debbie found that Tuffy progressed most rapidly when she divided his training into short segments. She felt that Tuffy got bored if required to repeat the same behavior too often. Veruccus's methods and results were different. After a week when he had made little progress with Dash's training, he suggested that the dolphin was sick. "A rat would have learned this by now," he complained. "Look," said Veruccus, standing by the pool. "His head is not symmetrical. The blowhole seems to be off to the left of center and not quite level. Perhaps he has had brain damage."

I took Veruccus to my office and showed him a dolphin skull, pointing out that the premaxillary fossae, plates of bone that lie just under the dolphin's blowhole, are twice as large on the right side. It is a little like a deformed human nose, with a large nostril on the right and a smaller one on the left. I also showed him papers by anatomists and cetologists that explained the asymmetry of the dolphin's skull. I don't think Veruccus paid much attention to my discussion, but after seeing the published papers, he was reluctantly convinced. He insisted, however, that I conduct a thorough physical examination of Dash.

I did the examination. We found that Dash had grown considerably, gaining almost a hundred pounds since his first days at Pacific Ocean Park. We also ran blood tests and a urinalysis, and we took Dash to the Point Mugu dispensary for x-rays. At the dispensary we were asked not to come back during working hours. Our dolphin x-raying had caused disruption and broken some equipment. There also was a minor injury: When a careless corpsman threw a protective x-ray apron over my helper Growth, he had mussed Growth's hair.

When I finished the examination of Dash, I reported my findings to Veruccus. Nothing was wrong. The psychologist was skeptical but polite. "Kew for going to all the trouble," he said in clipped tones. He apparently had hit upon a means of saving energy by this abbreviated speech.

For another week Dash resisted learning the white rat intelligence tests. Veruccus, frustrated, now suggested that my medical examination had put Dash off. Woody pointed out that the psychological tests were visual, thus all wrong for dolphins. In response, Veruccus modified his approach. He made larger plywood symbols and put them on levers to be suspended in the water. Dash was lackadaisical. He swam forward to touch one or the other of the symbols. If, perhaps by accident, he chose correctly, he won a fish. If wrong, no fish. Failing the first time, the animal would hit the same symbol harder.

During the same period Debbie had made good progress in her work with Tuffy. She spent several hours each day in the water with the dolphin. Carrying a fish bucket over her arm, she stroked and petted the dolphin before putting on the blinders. Blowing a police whistle immediately when the dolphin completed a task correctly, she rewarded Tuffy with fish from the bucket, then stroked him some more. We often heard it repeated around the facility that Debbie's gentle method had worked a miraculous change in Tuffy.

Veruccus noticed her success, but he did not, at first, show it. Confident of his own methods, he appeared suspicious of ideas originated by others. Therefore, I was surprised one day to see Veruccus in a new wet suit on his way toward Dash's pool, carrying a small stepladder in one hand and a yellow plastic bucket in the other. It appeared to me that he was preparing to test Debbie's technique. Curious, I followed along to observe.

Veruccus ascended his little ladder to the top of the pool wall, which stood about four feet above the ground. Resting the yellow bucket on the pool's edge, he balanced himself there. In preparation for his entry, the water level in the pool had been lowered to a depth of about two feet. The psychologist perched on the thin steel rim of the pool and sat for a moment. Undoubtedly, he sat in comfort, since his arctic wet suit had three-eighths of an inch of padding. I noticed that he wore a police whistle around his neck and that his plastic bucket contained Dash's usual day's ration of fifteen pounds of smelt. I also noticed that the pool had not been cleaned in several days. A thin film of slippery dark green algae covered the walls. Dash was swimming in slow circles in the shallow, murky water. The dolphin's dorsal fin appeared strangely sharklike above the surface.

Finally Veruccus jumped in, drew the bucket down after him, and waded, slipping a little, to the center of the pool. He bent over and dangled a tiny smelt in the water. Dash started swimming faster. This got the water swirling in the tank, creating a small wave that made the water deeper at the edge of the circular pool where Dash swam and shallow in the center where Veruccus stood. Dash ignored the fish Veruccus proffered. As the animal swam in circles, the flexible pool walls creaked and bent. Ignoring a life's history of frequent falls, I mounted Veruccus's stepladder for a better view.

From this precarious perch, I saw Dash suddenly turn on his side and like an alligator closing on its prey, spread his jaws wide. I'm not sure whether it was the three-hundred-pound dolphin or the several hundred gallons of water directed at the center of the pool by the animal's maneuver that knocked Veruccus flat, but when I managed to get untangled from my overturned stepladder and stand up, I saw Veruccus sitting with a dazed expression in the water at the far edge of the pool. Dash was busily gobbling the scattered smelt.

Veruccus eventually retreated to an observation post atop the poolside trailers. From here he could oversee all our pools and observe our dolphins. At first Veruccus on his perch attracted attention, but everyone soon got used to him there, and most of the time the staff went about their chores without noticing him at all.

On one occasion Veruccus's ladder and rooftop perch proved handy for me. It was one of those long California afternoons just past the summer solstice. Working late and alone at the facility about 7 P.M., I heard a loud staccato chirping. I could see a dolphin's head above a blue plastic pool. Moving closer, I saw Dash with his head held high above the water, balancing with his tail flukes on the pool bottom. The animal's snout pointed skyward, and his eyes were closed; he stood upright on his flukes. As he chirped, Dash rocked from side to side on his flukes, making slow forward progress across the pool. After two or three minutes of this behavior, the dolphin exhaled with a snort and fell on his side. This was something I had never seen before. I climbed onto the roof of the trailer next to the pools so I could observe all the dolphins without disturbing them. Now on the pool bottom, Dash lay motionless on his left side.

In the next tank Tuffy took up the staccato chirping, using the same stance and motion. The top of his flukes, bent under, rested squarely on the tank bottom. As he rocked from side to side, inching forward, his upper body stood out of the water to flipper level.

Dash surfaced, and the two dolphins began a chirping duet in their adjacent tanks. Both stood upright in the water, walking clumsily around in a penguinlike gait. In unison they snorted and crashed to the pool bottom, where both lay on their left side. Their eyes were closed or nearly so in air, but both dolphins had the upper, right eye open underwater, as if to look at something in the air. Occasionally, each would exhale a bubble that rose in a silver baseball-size oval to the surface. After almost three minutes on the bottom, the dolphins arose to repeat the standing-walking-singing act.

The last episode ended quickly when Doris noticed me from her pool. She snorted and swam rapidly around the pool, splashing water over the sides. Quitting their strange routine, Dash and Tuffy lay on the surface, looking up toward my perch.

I don't know what Dash and Tuffy were doing with their strange behavior. But if the dolphins wanted to imitate humans walking, talking, and lying on the sand, they could not have done it much better. The humans that came around our tanks did not lie down, but the facility was adjacent to a beach, and the dolphins had an opportunity to watch sunbathers. A far-fetched explanation? Perhaps. I have thought of other possibilities for this behavior, which is by no means common, although I have since seen it in other dolphins, male and female. The clumsy walking and chirping possibly was a good sea gull imitation. (Later Dash was observed to catch a sea gull from time to time.) Or maybe this behavior is something that dolphins do on rare occasions in shallow water, motivated by something we humans cannot comprehend. Perhaps it is just play.

I often have wondered whether the dolphins' play

had anything to do with what happened a few days later. The day before the Fourth of July I arrived at work just as the sun's first rays appeared over the mountains to the east of Point Mugu. Expecting a busy day of paperwork, I planned to have a quick look at each animal, then go right to my desk.

All was well in the main pool. Playful, Doris butted a volleyball at me. The spinning, dripping, algae-covered oval squirted through my outstretched hands, striking just above the waist, leaving a grapefruit-size splotch of green algae on my blue shirt. Pausing only to kick the ball to the opposite side of the pool, I continued on my way and was out of range by the time the dolphin retrieved the ball. She held the white sphere between her flippers as she swam, using the ball's buoyancy to lift her up for a better view of my activities.

Dash peered at me in his usual suspicious manner from the first plastic pool, but Tuffy's pool was empty. I rushed over. The far wall had collapsed, and Tuffy was nowhere in sight. A gully led from a large mud puddle at the pool's edge right down to the lagoon. The plastic pool had ruptured, and water rushing out apparently had swept the dolphin with it. Had Tuffy escaped?

The next pool also was empty of water, but I was relieved to see Salty on the plastic bottom. He arched his back and lifted his snout toward me. Although he lay in two or three inches of water that puddled on the pool bottom, his back was dry.

As I uncoiled a water hose to give Salty a refreshing splash, I heard a snort from the wreckage of Pool 2, near the mud puddle. Dropping the hose, I bounded over in time to glimpse Tuffy's snout above the surface of the opaque muddy water. His body was trapped under the metal wall that had collapsed. The dolphin reached just high enough for his blowhole to clear the water and took a labored breath before settling back to the bottom of the puddle. I tried to lift the mass of metal and plastic off the animal, but Tuffy was caught in the hole that had split the pool wall.

Holding the wreckage as high as possible to allow Tuffy a little more room to breathe, I pondered what to do next. About 150 feet away, Ensign Frank Harvey entered the facility, walking quietly and deliberately toward inspection. The white scrubbed face of a New Yorker not yet tanned by the California sun offered a marked contrast to his immaculate dark coat, tie, and pants. Frank wore the face of one awakened too early to accept the invasion of outside stimuli on his senses. He started when I yelled his name.

Frank placed his notebook and cap on a clean space of concrete apron, then skipped on mirror-shiny black shoes across the sand to me. "You hold this up while I try to pull the dolphin out," I told him.

While Frank lifted the pool wall, I grappled in the muddy water for a hold on the dolphin. Straddling Tuffy's head, up to my knees in the puddle, I reached backward to grasp the slippery, streamlined body. Finding the base of the flippers—the dolphin's armpits—I pulled. Tuffy began to flounce from side to side, wiggle, and stroke his tail. Coffee-colored grit shot up in the air. When I managed to wipe the grit from my eyes and look up, I saw muddy water dribbling off Frank's carefully combed sandy hair.

Tuffy's snout rested on moist sand at the far end of the mud puddle. The blowhole cleared, Frank and I stood over the dolphin, puffing from the effort but ready to grasp the dolphin if he tried to flop back into the danger zone. Bill Scronce arrived, and the three of us lifted Tuffy onto a green army stretcher and carted him over to the edge of the main pool. As we tilted the stretcher so Tuffy could roll into clean seawater, he joined Doris and the other dolphins in a race across the pool, then swam back, open-mouthed, eyes on us as we carted Salty across to join them.

I never learned what caused the rupture that led to Tuffy's almost drowning in the muddy water under the pool wreckage. Perhaps it *was* the dolphins' rough-housing. This was the second such escape for Tuffy. The first time I had seen him endangered by the wet sheet covering his blowhole during transport, and just in time I had pulled the cloth free so he could breathe. Twice now he had escaped accidental injury or death. I hoped that the proverbial "third thing" never would occur.

6

After Tuffy's pool collapsed, Debbie was uncertain how he would respond to her training. Five other dolphins would be in the pool, and she knew that the dominant animal in a group often insisted on being the first in line for food, making it difficult to dispense rewards. But Tuffy left no doubt about who was dominant. The scars along Tuffy's body and his past behavior were ample testimony to his scrappy nature. Although Salty was larger, Tuffy lorded it over the group as soon as he entered the pool. The other dolphins kept a safe distance later that day when Debbie came to the edge of the pool with her fish bucket.

Although Tuffy immediately retrieved the weighted ring when she threw it in the new pool, Debbie decided to give the dolphin some time to adapt to the crowded situation before trying anything new. Compounding her problems, a diver now entered the pool to do some filming. Tuffy swam close to the whining camera, moved his head from side to side, and turned upside down and on his side, examining the camera from every angle with his sonar. I was pleased with his response to the diver, since Tuffy would have to perform before a diver's camera in the film with Glenn Ford and later we would use divers in some of our experiments.

By the end of the training session, Tuffy was back in form, going through the hoops only when Debbie commanded with the beeper. Watching this, I was relieved to see how well Tuffy had handled the stress. Considering that he must have gone through the dolphin equivalent of the great California earthquake at 6 A.M. that day when his pool collapsed, his shift to performing in the main pool in the presence of a human diver and other dolphins had gone extremely well.

A few days later an unexpected setback occurred. Dash was moved into the main pool, while the other dolphins went back to individual pools for project work. From the standpoint of the overall research objectives, the move was prudent. From the standpoint of Debbie's work with Tuffy, the trade was not good.

For two days the trainer made no progress. When Tuffy approached, Dash came along as well, ever ready to compete for fish thrown to Tuffy for reward. On the following day the pump broke and the water level was low all day. Debbie could do little work, and the dolphins were left to their own devices.

Tuffy and Dash spent much of the afternoon swimming rapidly around the pool next to the wall to build up a wave against its surface. Then they coasted on the wave, much as Dash had done to steal the smelt from Veruccus. Both dolphins enjoyed this sport. I watched Tuffy going at great speed just under the surface. The faster he swam, the larger the wave became. Then, perhaps because Dash had tired of generating his own waves, he skittered in just ahead of Tuffy. The shared wave dissipated in ten or twelve feet and ended in a dolphin fight.

Tuffy screeched. The water churned as the animals flailed, rasped, and slapped at each other. A flipper emerged between two gray jaws and disappeared as a pair of flukes surfaced and groped for balance and momentum. I tried to keep track of the large crescent scar as the gray bodies twisted and turned for an instant above the surface.

Finally, the fight broke into a chase. Around the perimeter, then cutting across, the lead dolphin darted this way and that, trying to avoid his pursuer's teeth. As one dolphin leaped high out of the water and the other followed with snapping jaws, I could see the semicircular scar, like a large horseshoe, on the dolphin in pursuit. Tuffy owned the pool. After that day, Dash kept a respectful distance when Debbie came to work.

Toward the end of July there was a period of clear water, and Glenn Ford and the movie crew came to film Tuffy's sonar demonstration. The animal performed almost flawlessly. Wearing the blinders, creaking and pulsing as he swam, the dolphin glided through the hoop maze and retrieved the weighted ring from anywhere in the pool; he repeated it again and again for the cameras. Everyone seemed pleased. But with Tuffy nothing was completely predictable. As Ford stood by the main pool, Tuffy suddenly splashed a gallon of seawater on him. Dripping wet, the actor had to change to a dry uniform to go on with the film.

Despite such occasional pranks, Tuffy continued to progress. His successes nurtured my continuing dream of having a trained dolphin free and untethered in the open ocean. I decided to discuss my plans with Woody. I had learned that Woody was almost always skeptical of a new idea when it was first presented. "How will you control the animal in the lagoon?" Woody insisted. "What if he becomes frightened or too confused to respond? What are you going to do if the animal simply wanders away?" But in the end I saw that Woody was as eager for an open-ocean trained dolphin as I was. He agreed that if Debbie could get the dolphin to wear a harness and leash, we could take a shot at working with Tuffy in the lagoon.

We took Tuffy out of the water to take measurements. We decided on a harness consisting of three straps encircling the dolphin's body: one just forward of the flippers, another just behind them, and a third just behind the dorsal fin. The three circles would be connected by a single strap on each side running along midbody. Marty, who had experience rigging parachutes, obtained the material from the parachute loft at Point Mugu and sewed up the harness to Tuffy's specifications. In short order Debbie had a harness with which to practice.

I was concerned that we should go slowly, as Woody had cautioned. A bad experience with the harness could send Tuffy back to the bad-boy behavior so common just a few months before. Debbie began by having the dolphin retrieve the harness to get him accustomed to the feel of the material. He learned this quickly, but the next step, the placement of a single strap around the dolphin behind his flippers, took a good deal more time. Nevertheless, by early August Debbie had Tuffy wearing the entire harness; by the middle of the month he would follow her around on a leash like an obedient dog. Quickly, she got him to follow her lead into a lifting sling. I could hardly believe it. The sling had been used to lift Tuffy to numerous unpleasant experiences: examinations, blood collecting, moves to strange places. Yet now the dolphin readily entered the sling, which was essential for the experiments I had planned.

Until now Debbie had harnessed Tuffy only with the water level lowered so she could wade on the bottom. Now she switched to harnessing the dolphin from the side of the pool at full water depth. We also had divers go into the pool and feed the dolphin underwater. Mistakenly, I began to think there was no limit to what Debbie could do with Tuffy. I suggested that to prepare for future eventualities, she should leave the dolphin tied by his leash to a davit at the pool's edge for a few minutes. Later we would have to tether the dolphin to a small boat by his leash. She lowered the water to waist level, harnessed Tuffy, and had him retrieve in harness and leash a few times. Then she threw the leash line up so I could fasten it to the edge and climbed out of the pool.

Tuffy apparently liked neither the tether nor Debbie's departure. He pulled on the line, flounced around, and snapped at the lanyard; then he went into a pout, his forehead pressed hard against the concrete tank wall. After a minute Debbie pitched him a fish. It fell near his jaw, and the dolphin gobbled it in usual form. A minute later the dolphin took another fish. Some of his tension appeared to ease.

Tuffy seemed calm ten minutes later when we untied the tether and Debbie went back into the pool. She used the leash to pull the dolphin toward her. As the passive, almost immobile, dolphin touched her body at waist level, Debbie reached over to remove the leash. But Tuffy had been playing possum. Suddenly he drew his head back and lashed at Debbie, banging her in the ribs with his snout. This is something pigs do fairly often; the closest human equivalent is a slap with the back of the hand. As he repeated the strike, Debbie cried out and fell back against the pool wall. I was about to jump in and try to rescue her when Tuffy relaxed again and drifted away. An hour later we called Tuffy over and removed his harness. His behavior appeared to have returned to normal, but Debbie walked around for several days with bruised ribs.

Four days later we began to get Tuffy used to working from a boat. Debbie fed him from a dinghy in the pool, harnessed him from the boat, had him swim into the sling held beside the boat, and had him retrieve on his leash and return to her while she sat in the boat. Next we towed the dinghy around the edge of the pool, with Debbie seated in it, leading Tuffy along by the leash. Only one more thing had to be done before we were ready to take Tuffy to the lagoon. We needed a sound-producing device that the dolphin would come to anytime he was called. This homing signal had to produce a sound distinctive from the beeper that signaled the dolphin to go on his hoop run. It had to be reliable, inexpensive, and capable of projecting sound a considerable distance through water.

The engineers told us that solutions were simple, but they all were expensive. I was discussing the problem with Debbie when Marty came over to introduce a chief petty officer who had recently taken over the aircrew survival training at Point Mugu. "What about the new pilot rescue beacon?" asked the chief.

"If you are talking about the new orange beacon for the life vest, I've seen it flash," said Marty, "but we need something that makes sound loud enough for a submerged dolphin to hear a hundred yards away."

"The strobe that you've seen produces a sharp click with each flash of light," the chief explained. "From what I've heard about these dolphins' keen sense of hearing, they might be able to hear the beacon a hundred yards through the water. I'll drop one by, and you can test it."

Debbie immediately started teaching Tuffy to come to the signal. The dolphin quickly learned to seek out the strobe and touch it with his snout, but since the main pool was less than twenty yards across, the exercise was hardly an adequate test of Tuffy's response.

On the last day of August we decided to test Tuffy in the lagoon. From the small boat in the main pool Debbie harnessed Tuffy, led him into the lifting sling, and adjusted his flippers to be sure they were tucked straight back along his body. Positioned badly, one of the dolphin's flippers could be broken during the lift. We lifted Tuffy with the hand winch and laid him on a foam-rubber pad in a pickup, then trucked him down to the north lagoon.

Although Tuffy's response to the strobe had been prompt and reliable in the pool, I was not confident that the dolphin would stick around when we turned him loose in the lagoon. A short distance north of our pools, an old wooden causeway, condemned for foot or vehicle traffic, reached across the lagoon, dividing it into northern and southern halves. Standing in the shallows on black pilings spaced in pairs, the aged causeway reminded me of a procession of giant jungle ants. A dolphin trying to escape to the sea might view it as a barrier, I hoped.

On the northern side of the causeway we found an expanse of moderately deep water next to the new concrete bridge. There we could exercise Tuffy behind three barriers: the shallows that turned to mud flats at low tide, the old causeway, and the lagoon mouth on the southern side with its shallows and crashing surf. Debbie snapped a leash about three feet long with a large yellow float on the end to Tuffy's harness. With the float we could keep track of the dolphin, and we reasoned that it might make the animal feel he was tethered even when he was free in the lagoon.

We put the boat in the water, and then Bill Scronce, Marty, Debbie, and I lifted the animal in his sling and waded into muddy, waist-deep water. We lowered the sling, submerging the pole that held up one side, and pulled the canvas away from the dolphin. Even though he was free of the sling, Tuffy stayed beside the canvas as if waiting for us to do something more. Debbie pulled on Tuffy's harness, tugging him toward deeper water. For an instant the dolphin seemed almost paralyzed, but when Debbie pushed him away toward the bridge, Tuffy rolled over and took off.

Tuffy swam toward the concrete bridge, cruising the deep water along its length. Then he turned to look toward Debbie, who sat in the little boat preparing to call for his return. After a brief pause the dolphin headed toward the old wooden causeway. I could see the yellow float bob and waggle about fifty yards away as the dolphin picked up speed.

I started worrying in earnest. I thought of all the work we had put into training and caring for the dolphin. I wondered whether the float and harness attached to Tuffy could endanger him if he strayed. I wondered about the tide and the water depth under the causeway. With sinking heart I told myself I should have planned the first release for a lower tide. Just then, about one hundred yards away, the yellow float plopped on end and changed direction. In less than a minute Tuffy was back. He cruised by Debbie's boat, keeping an eye on her but ignoring her call. Does he know she is going to snap the long leash back on him? I wondered. As if on a lark, Tuffy continued to swim around the lagoon.

For about fifteen minutes I fidgeted as Tuffy continued his exploration. When he finally came back to Debbie, he took a fish and allowed her to attach his leash to the yellow float. Debbie tossed the weighted ring into the brown water, and Tuffy waited obediently beside the boat until she signaled him to go get it. As he returned the ring, we saw mud from the lagoon bottom clinging to Tuffy's snout.

Tuffy lay still in the water beside the small boat, seeming to ignore everyone except Debbie. We positioned him in the sling for the return trip to the pool. The test in the lagoon had been short, less than half an hour, but we were jubilant about the day's work.

After two more successful trips to the enclosed north lagoon, I decided it was safe to work with Tuffy in the main lagoon. The navy had almost finished building a pontoon enclosure in the lagoon for the dolphins. We could walk from the main pool area, down a row of pontoons 6 feet wide to a point about 120 feet into the lagoon where the water was 15 or 20 feet deep.

Debbie harnessed Tuffy and led him into the sling as usual. We carried him down the pontoons and winched him down into the water beside the dinghy where Debbie waited. Marty started the outboard on the Boston Whaler, a small boat that was to tow the dinghy out into the lagoon with Tuffy swimming alongside. The dolphin seemed undisturbed by the engine noise, but about two hundred yards into the lagoon several salt-and-pepper-spotted harbor seals stretched their necks to peer at our strange procession, and Tuffy lingered behind the boat. Marty cut the engine to idle. From the Whaler we watched as Debbie tugged on the leash to bring Tuffy toward us, but the dolphin apparently was startled by the seals and pulled in the opposite direction, splashing and fighting against the harness.

Fearing that either the harness or the leash might break, Bill released the towline. Debbie still held the leash, though, and Tuffy towed the dinghy for about a hundred yards back toward the pontoons, then began to circle. We watched as the little boat turned around and around. Debbie tried calling the dolphin, but he would not respond. She tried throwing fish in his direction, but he would not take them. After about ten minutes the dolphin slowed down a little. Bill grabbed a handful of fish, jumped into the water, and swam about twenty feet until the dolphin came toward him to take a fish from his outstretched hand; then for several minutes Tuffy cruised back and forth between Bill in the water and Debbie in the boat, taking a fish at each end of the circuit. Finally, Marty restarted the engine of the Whaler, and as we towed the dinghy back in, Tuffy followed along. At the pontoons Tuffy swam into the sling without hesitation and waited motionlessly for a ride back to his pool.

Each day Debbie repeated the training procedure, working with Tuffy for a time in the main pool, then harnessing him and leading him into the sling for transport to the lagoon. Sometimes Tuffy refused to wear the harness, and Debbie soon figured out a way to punish him for this misbehavior. The two Lags in the pool were tame now, and when Tuffy was disobedient, Debbie tossed one of his fish to a Lag. The black-and-white dolphin grabbed the food and sped away. Tuffy had learned that he could not catch the sleek little dolphins, and after a few fish went to the Lags, Tuffy cooperated and Debbie harnessed him without difficulty.

That Tuffy tolerated the harness at all is remarkable. Perhaps no animal is more ill-suited for a harness than a dolphin. Its smooth, spindle-shaped body is structured to cut through the water with a minimum of resistance. As a swimmer and sometime bodysurfer, I could imagine the feeling of water drag the harness created on a speeding dolphin.

On my trips to sea with Mo to catch the Lags, I had marveled at their power and grace as they played about the bow of our boat. Dr. Tom Lang, our hydrodynamics expert, had measured bottlenosed dolphins swimming as fast as seventeen miles per hour for a very brief period, and with the help of dolphin experts Kenneth Norris and Karen Pryor, Dr. Lang had induced a Hawaiian dolphin to swim about twenty-five miles per hour for less than two seconds. (Sustained dolphin traveling speeds were much slower.) On the trips with Mo, we also encountered Dall porpoises that could overtake our boat at twenty miles per hour.

Dalls are short muscular animals with small black heads that taper smoothly back to a stocky chest, where a striking white belly patch curves up in a crescent along each side. The Dalls often swam so fast that the water did not clear their stubby heads as they surfaced to breathe. Their explosive breath threw water three or four feet into the air in a characteristic spout and trail we came to call a rooster tail. One afternoon as we were heading home at full power, I saw a pair of rooster tails off to my left, about three hundred yards off our port bow. A few seconds later a small group of Dalls raced to overtake our boat, and soon three were riding the bow wave. The three Dalls then pulled ahead of our speeding craft and disappeared under the waves. I ran up to the wheel house to check the shaft speed on our two propellers and then estimated the porpoises' top speed at between twenty-five and thirty miles per hour.

There are more than thirty species of the small, powerful toothed whales that we call porpoises or dolphins. I use an imprecise number, "more than thirty," because I am not sure exactly how many species there are. Some taxonomists (we call them "lumpers") argue for putting similar animals together in one species, while others (we call them "splitters") tend to erect another species with the slightest variation in an animal's form or structure. What's more, there may be other species that scientists simply have not found. For example, between 1963 and 1973, a decade during which humans walked on the moon and brought back photographs and rocks for study, three dolphin species were photographed and studied in the flesh for the first time by scientists.

At first it seemed absurd to me that mammals that

grow to several hundred pounds in weight and live in herds could go unrecognized and essentially unknown for so long. But as Mo and I cruised around the Channel Islands, looking for dorsal fins above whitecaps, I began to understand the frustration of biologists who study dolphins at sea. Many groups were difficult to approach. We could see the dolphins well only when they played about our boat's bow, and then we looked down on their backs for only a minute or two before they were gone. Most of their lives were spent below the waves and hidden from our view. Late one afternoon, when the crew of sailors who manned our craft was tired and itching to head for port, one of the sailors coined a name for me: Dr. Seymour Fishback. "Doc, you want to see more fish backs than anybody has a need to," the young sailor exclaimed.

On ten consecutive days in mid-September we exercised Tuffy in the lagoon. We encountered harbor seals several times, but Tuffy now ignored seals as well as occasional powerboats that happened by. Still, there were setbacks. Sometimes, for no apparent reason, the animal balked at following the boat. Sometimes he refused to swim back into the sling at the end of an exercise. Debbie was patient, however. On such occasions she waited for a few minutes until the dolphin decided to follow her commands. Then she went on with the work. Soon Debbie could remove the leash and signal Tuffy to retrieve the ring from the bottom almost anywhere in the lagoon. The dolphin would swim back and forth between Debbie and a diver until Debbie called Tuffy with the strobe at distances of one hundred feet or more.

Unfortunately, Debbie's temporary assignment as a dolphin trainer was coming to an end. Soon she was to start graduate school at Stanford, and I wondered how we would fare with Tuffy without her gentle touch. On Debbie's last day we moved Tuffy into a new permanent residence in the pontoon pens. When Debbie removed Tuffy's harness at the end of the day, she lingered, stroking the dolphin and saying an affectionate good-bye.

One of the great things about the small field of dolphin science in the 1960s was that I soon came to know, or feel that I knew, almost all the active cetacean scientists in the world. Of course, I had met only a few of these men and women, but I had read their articles, written them letters to ask questions, and frequently enjoyed their replies. Several of these scientists were connected with the oceanographic institution at Woods Hole, Massachusetts, and prominent among them was the husband and wife team of Barbara Lawrence and William Schevill. I was thrilled when Bill Schevill answered my first letter, "Welcome to the porpoise business." On another occasion, when a local scientist asked me whether I knew another Woods Hole scientist, Dr. John Kanwisher, I replied "yes" without thinking because I knew his work so well. Then I realized I was mistaken; I had never met the man.

Unexpectedly, I did meet the noted Dr. Kanwisher

when he showed up one morning unannounced at my office door. My first impression was of a man of wiry build, with short-cropped hair that stuck straight up as if a cartoonist had sketched it to express intense excitement. This tall, vibrant man carried a large, battered suitcase. John was on his way back from the Galápagos, or Peru, or Mexico, or some other exotic place that I can't recall, where he had been measuring the metabolism of some rare cactus or recording the heartbeat of a hummingbird.

Within two minutes of his arrival John had opened his suitcase on the floor in the middle of my office. As far as I could see, the only clothes in the case were a change of underwear and some knitted socks wrapped around a wallet. Most of the voluminous case was stuffed with electronic gear and gas analysis equipment. As he showed me the tiny transmitters and electrodes, all of which he had built himself, John spoke in staccato bursts of words. He radiated an electrifying excitement about his work with plants and animals. As I was to learn later, his scientific background had been in the physical sciences rather than in biology. Nevertheless, John was fascinated by all forms of life and constantly tried to work out unsolved puzzles in biological function.

Later that morning as we strode along the shore of Mugu Lagoon, I had to run to keep up with him. Meanwhile, I tried to explain our work with Tuffy and how we hoped to collect physiological data on the dolphin diving free in the open sea. Speeding along like a child let loose in a toy store, John did not seem to pay a great deal of attention to my explanations. He kept saying, "Look at that" or "I didn't know those existed here." John marveled at the rich variety of bird and animal life, pointing with excitement at a brown pelican as it plunged out of the air into the water, at a huge guitarfish hovering over the rippled sandy bottom of the lagoon, at a procession of harbor seals that paused to stare back at us, and at numerous other creatures that I had too often taken for granted.

When we went to work with Tuffy, John saw us harness the dolphin and call Tuffy out into the lagoon. Now I could see that he was starting to take a new interest in my project. He stared in amazement as the trained dolphin swam first to one boat, then to another, and finally back to our station. Now he was excited. I imagined I could hear the crackle of sparks flying from his brain through the tips of his straight hair as he leaned forward to watch. "You must catch the dolphin's first breath after one of those dives," he exclaimed.

"We still have to train Tuffy for that," I replied.

"I can measure the oxygen and carbon dioxide in that breath with the Scholander half-cc [cubic centimeter] analyzer I have in my suitcase. We can take it right out in one of those little boats. I only need a half-cc," said John, holding his thumb and index finger a couple of millimeters apart.

John had heard my explanation after all. But I had to remind him that the dolphin-diving portion was just a plan. We would have to wait to see whether Tuffy cooperated with us in the open sea. Right there, we made a pact. "You figure out how to get a breath sample after the dolphin makes a deep ocean dive," he proposed, "and I'll be out on the first plane to analyze it."

In the years that followed I would see John Kanwisher many more times in California, but this first visit was

especially memorable. I was heartened by the knowledge that a "real" scientist thought my plans for Tuffy
were not only reasonable but very exciting.

With Debbie off to Stanford, we needed another trainer,
and I was happy to hire Wally three weeks later. Until
Wally began, Tuffy received less instruction than he
deserved. Both Bill Scronce and I had so many other
duties that our training time was limited. Several emer-
gencies also distracted my attention from Tuffy. One
that I recall vividly began when Bill Powell hurried
into my office with a piece of bad news. One of the
female dolphins, Doris, had swallowed a nail, maybe
several nails, Bill told me. This was especially worri-
some because Doris was the vital participant in an
important sonar experiment. During recent construc-
tion around her pool, some nails had fallen into the
tank, and predictably, the inquisitive dolphin had picked
up a few.

Bill had seen Doris earlier carrying a shiny nail in
her mouth. By the time he called her, proffered a fish,
and tried to reach for the nail, it had disappeared.
Later he saw Doris mouthing a rusty nail, and quickly
he held a fish high above the dolphin so she would
open her mouth. With his free hand he reached for the
nail, and since Doris liked to have her tongue rubbed,
this strategy should have worked. But just as his fingers reached the scalloped edge of her tongue—slurp,
the nail disappeared.

I had an idea about how to get the nails out, provided they were still in Doris's first stomach compartment. I had learned a technique in veterinary school
for removing hardware from the first stomach of a

cow. First the animal would be fed a magnet; then the magnet, with the swallowed hardware attached, would be retrieved. To succeed with this plan, I had to find the number and position of the nails Doris had swallowed before the pointed nails penetrated her stomach wall or damaged her intestine. I contacted the radiologist at St. John's Hospital in Oxnard. "Yes, glad to x-ray your dolphin," said Dr. William Fox. "Just bring her to emergency. We'll have pictures for you in no time."

We deposited Doris on a rubber pad in our navy pickup and sped off to St. John's. During the ride I saw no signs of blood in Doris's mouth or stool and no indication of pain in her abdomen. With my stethoscope I listened to her chest. Her heart chugged along at thirty-five beats per minute until she heaved for a breath; then the beat quickened to a one-hundred-per-minute rate for three or four seconds before resuming its previous slow pace—absolutely normal for a perfectly relaxed dolphin.

As we approached the hospital, Marty followed all the ambulance traffic arrows and backed us right up under the big sign that read EMERGENCY. As nurses helped us load Doris on a gurney with large rubber wheels, a half-dozen sister hats crowded around. Doris called almost continuously with her high-pitched, canarylike whistles as the nuns rushed the gurney down the hall toward x-ray, where Dr. Fox met us. He introduced himself to me with a business card bearing an x-ray picture of his own skull. Tall, thin, and balding, Dr. Fox stood smiling above the crowd. He had only to speak a word and assistants rushed to set up x-ray film cassettes and make exposures. Then we waited for the news. In a short time Dr. Fox summoned me into the darkroom. "Not my best radiograph," said Dr. Fox, "but the dolphin's problem is easy to identify."

With the film held up against a light, the radiograph reminded me of an x-ray of a small drawer in a carpenter's toolbox. It revealed three nails of different sizes, two washers, a screw, and an amorphous mass of somewhat less density. "Brillo," said Dr. Fox, as he outlined the amorphous image with his pen. "Yes," he mused, "definitely something like metal wool."

Hurriedly returning to Point Mugu, we placed Doris in her pool to wait in comfort while Marty and I constructed a device to remove the hardware from her forestomach. We found a strong, round magnet that would easily pick up and hold the items Doris had swallowed, but our largest stomach tube was not of sufficient diameter to hold the magnet. Marty found a smooth garden hose, cut out a six-foot section, and installed the magnet in one end.

Working as quickly as possible, we removed Doris from her pool and lay her on a table cushioned with thick foam rubber. Sailors and trainers draped themselves loosely over Doris to prevent the dolphin from thrashing about or falling off the table during the operation. Marty and our intellectual sailor Gates clutched towels that would be used to hold the dolphin's jaws open. Then I noticed that the magnet was rough on the end. This was a problem. We did not want to risk tearing the dolphin's throat.

Running my fingers over the magnet, I thought out loud: "I need something smooth and soft to cover the magnet, something that will protect the dolphin's throat, something that will go down smoothly." Immediately, Gates opened his wallet and without a word handed me an ideal piece of latex rubber. Fitting the condom over the magnet, I secured it to the hose with a rubber band and covered the latex with surgical lubricant. The rubber-covered magnet was about half the size of a mackerel and just as slippery. Maybe Doris will swallow it as if it were a fish, I thought.

At a touch of my finger at the corner of her mouth, Doris opened her jaw. Marty slid in his towel and looped it around her upper jaw. Gates put his towel around her lower jaw. Both men pulled with just enough pressure to keep the rows of teeth about six inches apart. Their job was critical to me because the dolphin's ninety-six sharp teeth surrounded my arm as I reached into her mouth. As gently as possible, I placed the magnet into her throat and pushed it past the larynx; it slid down the esophagus and into the stomach. I let the contraption settle, then rotated its end so the magnet moved slightly inside the dolphin's stomach. Then, slowly and cautiously, I withdrew the hose. I imagined a crayfish on the opposite end, grasping gingerly with outstretched claws at my bait. Just as the magnet cleared her larynx, Doris struggled and snorted. I jerked on the hose. The magnet slithered out with three nails and a washer attached. The dolphin's sharp teeth had shredded the first latex cover, so Gates produced two more rubbers. This time I double-layered the latex, and soon we were ready for another go. The second trip into Doris's stomach went even more easily than the first. We retrieved another washer and a green, smelly lump: a scrubbing pad entwined with a screw.

Only a few minutes after we returned the dolphin to her pool, Doris hungrily gobbled smelt. She seemed little affected by her experience, and when I examined her again the following day, I found no sign of injury. Marty ran into a little difficulty, however. "You know that carton of rubbers you asked me to order to replace the ones you borrowed from Gates?"

"Sure," I replied. "I hope we never have to do this again, but we ought to have a few on hand just in case."

"Well, in the future you should be the one to take the requisition up to our supply department. Every one of those ladies read it. They kept giggling and reading the last words you wrote on the form: 'In case of emergency.' "

After the crisis with Doris was over, we were able to work with Tuffy again. On the morning we began, a warm, dry east wind was blowing. Since the sea was calm and the lagoon water was unusually clear, we worked until late afternoon. After quitting time I stood near Pen C watching Tuffy. As I had hoped, he soon turned to one of his favorite diversions.

The activity involved a fish, a kelp bass, colored in shades of brown and gray for camouflage. The large eyes of the bass seemed alert, suggesting greater sensibilities than those of the average lagoon fish. But the fish was no match for Tuffy in speed or cunning; the dolphin was three hundred times as large. As several kelp bass swam through the dolphin's enclosure, Tuffy moved his head sharply down and to the left, seizing one of the fish between his powerful jaws.

Since Tuffy had eaten his daily ration of seventeen pounds of mackerel and smelt, he was not hungry. For him the bass was not food but a toy. Tuffy carried the bass lightly in his jaws; the fish's tail stuck out on one side of his mouth and the head on the other. When the bass struggled, flexing its body and pumping its gills rapidly, Tuffy came to a stop in the center of his pen and slowly opened his jaws. The fish struggled away from the pointed pegs of ivory that gripped its body. Tail bent to one side, swimming haltingly, the injured bass lurched toward the netting of Tuffy's enclosure. An instant before the bass reached freedom, Tuffy seized it again. Carrying the fish in his jaws, Tuffy swam about the pen, squealing in apparent glee.

Like a cat toying with a mouse, Tuffy played with the bass until finally the limp, lifeless fish sank to the bottom. Then the dolphin retrieved the tattered corpse and towed it along, letting it slide in and out of his mouth until it was held together by a few strands of tissue. Tuffy let the remnant drop to the bottom, checking it from time to time as crabs came to pick morsels from it. I was fascinated by what seemed to be a cruel game, one the dolphin had not learned from humans.

As time passed I began to realize that in my musings about Tuffy, I often assumed that some intellectual process akin to human thought churned inside his gray head. Of course, I may have been guilty of allowing my emotions about the animal to cloud my perception and credit the animal with humanlike characteristics. Yet this anthropomorphic attitude is difficult to avoid when we observe and work with animals that we come to know as friends. We recognize much of ourselves in other animals, especially in mammals, which have warm, red blood, breathe air, bear live young, and nurse them on milk. Dolphins, like humans, possess highly convoluted brains, with a volume of cerebral cortex about 80 percent as large as our own. Moreover, the dolphin's smooth skin, perpetual smile, and exuberant behavior appeal to our human emotions. Based on my scientific knowledge and my intuition about dolphins, I could not help believing that some form of silent thought ticked behind Tuffy's large, alert eyes as he stared back at me from his world.

Although others shared my positive emotions about Tuffy, they were not convinced, as I was, that the dolphin could teach us something about his world. Viewing the evidence of the large dolphin brain as proof of the animal's special sensibilities and intelligence, some claimed that the animals must be left alone, that humans had no right to confine such creatures.

Nevertheless, I could argue, there was something to be said for Tuffy's relative safety from predators and his regular supply of food in captivity. To me the idyllic perfection of the dolphin's life in the sea was largely a fantasy. In reality dolphins lived a life constantly in search of food and at risk from parasites, disease, and predators. The scars on Tuffy's body were ample evidence that his earlier life in the sea had not been free of stress, and these scars were by no means the only imperfections on the dolphin's body. Various forms of dermatitis scored Tuffy's smooth, rubbery skin. When one mottled patch of skin healed, another discolored area soon appeared.

Tuffy's skin problem continued in captivity and worsened about the time Wally started as trainer, and although the dolphin had a hearty appetite, he did not look healthy. I had postponed a complete physical examination because I did not want the unpleasant tests to interrupt the dolphin's training, but as I looked at Tuffy's diseased skin, I realized we could wait no longer.

I began by injecting a local anesthetic under two of the nodules on Tuffy's skin. While we waited for the anesthetic to take effect, Growth, Gates, and several other sailors stood by to restrain the dolphin in case he chose to repel any of my ministrations. But Tuffy was a surprisingly good patient. He lay sideways, almost motionless on the pad. A moist sponge covered his uppermost eye to protect it from the bright sunlight.

While I treated Tuffy's sores, Gates recounted a story from an article he had just read reviewing tales of dolphins that had rescued drowning humans. The story concerned the poet and musician Arion, who lived in the seventh century B.C. Returning with rich profits from a tour of engagements across the sea, Arion was betrayed by the sailors whose vessel he had chartered. The sailors plotted to rob the musician, then throw him overboard. Arion made them welcome to his money but convinced his captors to allow one last musical performance, in full costume on the quarterdeck. At the end of his song, while his audience was still spellbound, Arion flung himself into the sea, where he was taken on the back of a dolphin and delivered safely to shore. As Gates's story went, the robbers were caught and Arion arrived home with his wealth restored—all because of a kind dolphin.

While I opened each lesion on Tuffy's body with a surgical scalpel, the sailors continued trading tales. I inserted a sterile cotton swab to collect bacteria; took some skin samples to examine under the microscope later; and cleaned each of the sores, applying antiseptic dye to prevent further infection. As I completed the examination, I injected Tuffy with an antibiotic and drew a tube of blood for laboratory testing.

Through all this slicing, poking, and probing, Tuffy lay calmly. By the time I had finished and we were carrying the dolphin back to the lagoon pen, Gates was instructing the group about Aristotle's studies of dolphins. Gates informed us that some twenty-five hundred years ago Aristotle had observed, among other things, that dolphins nursed their young on milk, breathed air, made sounds, slept, and lived long lives of twenty-five or thirty years. Wordlessly, I hoped that Tuffy too would live a long life.

My laboratory analysis showed that Tuffy had a high white blood cell count, with numerous purple-stained cells called neutrophils, which indicated a bacterial infection. I gave Wally a supply of antibiotic tablets and told him to put the pills in Tuffy's fish early each morning and late each afternoon. During the day Wally continued to work with the dolphin in Mugu Lagoon. About two weeks later most of the skin sores had healed, and we started to make plans to take Tuffy to the ocean.

Because it would be difficult to move Tuffy back and forth from the pools to the sea, we got Mo to construct an ocean pen of netting about eighteen feet on a side and approximately ten feet deep. He suspended the pen from a twenty-foot square of four- by four-inch timbers with a sealed fifty-five-gallon oil drum at each corner. The four oil drums floated the timbers about eighteen inches above the water. In one corner of the structure Mo hung a small underwater platform on which Wally could stand when he harnessed Tuffy, and in one side of the netting pen he built a gate that could be tied up when the dolphin was inside and let down so Tuffy could swim out.

Some people to whom I showed the pen did not think it would last long in the ocean. But Mo had ridden out storms aboard small fishing boats in the Gulf of Alaska and had gone through typhoons with Halsey's fleet during World War II, and I figured he knew better than most what the ocean could do.

The pen's low profile also drew questions. Everyone who had watched a Marineland show knew that dolphins could jump twenty feet into the air. How could we expect a barrier only eighteen inches above the water to contain a dolphin? My answer was simple: The dolphin has to want to stay in.

The portable pen was set up in the lagoon a short distance from the pontoon enclosure. To train Tuffy to exit the pen, Bill Scronce, in diving gear, took Tuffy's leash and swam through the gate. From outside Wally called the animal with the strobe. The dolphin followed Bill through the hole and out into the lagoon to touch the strobe in Wally's hand. Then Bill swam into the portable pen, and Tuffy followed. By the end of the day Wally could call the dolphin in and out of the pen on his own.

Woody was surprised when I told him about how quickly Tuffy had learned to swim in and out through the gate. "Dolphins seem to have a fear of barriers," he said. "I've seen cases where it took a week or more to get a dolphin to swim through a gate." Soon Wally had trained Tuffy to swim beside the little boat in Mugu Lagoon without being tethered to the leash. Wally would throw Tuffy a fish every minute or so as the dolphin obediently followed along. In this way he took Tuffy to Seal Point, where harbor seals slept on a sandbar, and had him practice retrieving. Next he went to the creek bridge, then to Smith's Landing, and so on, until Wally was certain that Tuffy would perform in a variety of locations. Tuffy retrieved the ring from the lagoon bottom in any area and at any depth.

Each time Wally and his sailor assistants stopped somewhere to work with Tuffy, a single brown pelican alighted a short distance away. The bird kept a hopeful eye on the smaller dinghy and the bucket from which Wally plucked fish to reward the dolphin. The wild harbor seals kept their distance. Sometimes they poked their whiskered faces high above the surface to observe the two boats with Tuffy swimming along beside, but soon they would resume dozing at the surface with whiskers pointing skyward or dive to go about their daily activities.

During the university break between Christmas and New Year's Day, Debbie returned to Point Mugu for a visit. In her three-month absence our facility had grown considerably: A new concrete pool was in use; Tuffy now lived permanently in Mo's floating pen; and two new huts had been built to house experimental equipment.

When she arrived, Debbie found Wally in the trainer's shed washing Tuffy's harness and training gear. She asked for permission to play with the dolphin. "Sure," said Wally, "I'm through working him for today."

Debbie donned her wet suit and ran down to the pontoon enclosure. When she arrived, she saw that winter rains had filled the creek, carrying mud and silt into the lagoon. The water was chocolate-colored, but Debbie could tell from eddies stirring the surface that the dolphin was there. After about thirty seconds a gray form broke the surface to blow, then instantly dived again.

Debbie stepped on the ladder going down into the water and climbed down to stand at waist depth on the last rung. She splashed the water with her hand. That was sure to bring Tuffy over, she thought. But the animal continued to swim unseen beneath the surface, and Debbie could see no response in the eddies that formed on the opposite side of the pen.

As Debbie stood in the water, she could look across the steel pontoons to a smaller pen floating on oil drums out in the lagoon. The dolphin in that pen was jumping and landing on its side, splashing water high into the air. She could hear the animal snort and slap its tail repeatedly against the surface of the water in its excitement.

Debbie floated out into the center of the pen. She was puzzled. Tuffy always had seemed to like it when she swam with him. Sometimes he offered his dorsal fin so she could grasp it and be towed around the pool. Other times, he rolled upside down to have his belly rubbed, playfully butted her with his snout, or lightly grasped her elbow in his jaws. But today Debbie was ignored. Only an inch or two of the dolphin's forehead showed as he surfaced every twenty or thirty seconds to breathe.

After a quarter-hour of paddling around the pool pursuing the elusive dolphin, Debbie was thoroughly dejected. Tuffy doesn't remember me, she thought. As she walked along the pontoon walkway toward the trainer's hut, she once more noticed the aggravated dolphin out in the lagoon, treading water with its tail, squealing to attract attention. I'd better tell Wally something's wrong with that animal, Debbie thought, as she continued toward the hut. She was now a little sorry that she had returned for this short visit. Her dolphin work always had seemed full of joy, hope, and promise, and now she felt empty.

"Wally, he doesn't recognize me," Debbie said. "It's just not the same Tuffy. He swims around the edge, barely breaks the surface to blow, and avoids me completely. He never once came over to me."

"Well, he followed our boat most of the day. We went all over the lagoon. Maybe he's tired. Why don't you plan on trying again after the first training session tomorrow? But just in case, maybe I better get Doc to go down and look at him. He could be getting sick again. You know, he's had a lot of skin problems since you left in September."

"That's probably a good idea," said Debbie with a little more hope in her voice. "While you're at it, you should check on the dolphin out in the small pen in the lagoon. That dolphin seemed agitated."

"Small pen?" asked Wally with a puzzled expression. "There's only one."

"I mean when I was at Tuffy's pen in the pontoon enclosure, I could see a dolphin in a small pen floating on oil drums out in the lagoon."

"Tuffy isn't in the pontoon enclosure," said Wally. "He's in a small. . . ."

That's all Debbie heard. She was out the door, running at full speed toward the lagoon. She ran across the pontoons, past Tuffy's old pen with its shy occupant, and across a long wooden plank. Tuffy was halfway out of the water to meet Debbie as she stepped on the corner of his pen.

"It was hard to tell who was more excited, the girl

or the porpoise," said Wally. Debbie and Tuffy spent an exuberant hour renewing old acquaintances.

In general I was optimistic about the success of our project. Not only were the newest employees proving their excellence, but Mo's portable pen had passed the initial test—Tuffy stayed in it. Even when Tuffy apparently wanted out, he did not jump over the framework. "It's a curious thing," I said to Mo. "A deer can leap six or seven feet into the air, and we have to build a fence at least that high to hold him. The dolphin can leap fifteen feet over the water, and we need only an eighteen-inch fence to hold him."

Although I knew Wally was right when he said that Tuffy was ready for experiments in the open ocean, I also knew that we still needed the answer to one key question: How far away could the dolphin be and still hear the strobe? Answering this question required human-dolphin cooperation. Earlier, we had trained Tuffy to touch one strobe, collect his fish reward, and then move to a second strobe located across the enclosure. With the pontoons to walk on, two people easily were able to keep calling the dolphin back and forth between two different locations. In the lagoon, however, three boats were needed for this task, and we could not always round up three boats. Sometimes we had to post a volunteer in waist-deep water at Seal Point with a bucket of fish, a strobe, and a portable radio for receiving Wally's commands.

Getting experienced volunteers was more difficult now. Both Bill Scronce and Growth had received military transfer orders. Growth went overseas and Bill to Jacksonville. I would miss the big, quiet sailor who was the best dolphin tail-holder I ever knew, but I would miss Bill even more. Bill and Marty had been with our project since its inception. Both were excellent divers—Marty claimed to be the best in the world—and both men knew how to get almost anything done. Fortunately, Marty could stay on, and he became our key man in training the young sailors on whom we depended.

By setting up three stations and calling Tuffy randomly between these stations, we could be certain that the dolphin was responding to the strobe and not just guessing about where to go next. Day by day we gradually moved the stations farther apart. When the distance reached two hundred yards, I could not believe it. To hear the click of the device, I had to hold it near my ear. How could the dolphin hear it two hundred yards away?

Woody pointed out another factor that made this even more impressive: "The lagoon is full of snapping shrimp, mussels, and other marine life," he reminded us. "There is a background of noise from these small animals clicking in the lagoon. To discriminate the click, the dolphin must have sensitive, superbly tuned hearing."

During these same weeks Drs. Scott Johnson and Bill Evans, both experts in underwater acoustics, proved experimentally that dolphins do indeed have excellent hearing sensitivity, with a frequency span seven or eight times as broad as that of a human. Bill Evans took our strobe and made some measurements confirming that if Tuffy had hearing sensitivity similar to that of Scott's experimental animal, Salty, he should be able to hear the strobe from even farther than two hundred yards away under ideal conditions.

With renewed confidence, Wally and I pressed on in our work with Tuffy. By early February we had determined that Tuffy almost always responded to the strobe at a distance of 450 yards and sometimes at 550 yards but never at ranges of 600 to 700 yards. I reasoned that we could expect the dolphin to come to us when called from at least a quarter-mile away. We were ready to take Tuffy to the ocean.

8

The sun was bright and the sea calm on February 8, 1965, the day we chose to take Tuffy to sea for the first time. Wally harnessed the dolphin and guided Tuffy into the lifting sling. We carried him up to the main pool for one more preliminary test, of an acoustic telemetry device that had been built to send back Tuffy's heartbeat during a dive. Inside suction cups we molded flat silver electrodes like those used for recording the heartbeat of astronauts. Like plastic leeches, the cups gripped the dolphin's skin, insulating the electrodes from the conductive salts of seawater and holding them tight against the skin so the electrical signal of Tuffy's heart could be detected.

Wally attached the telemetry device, contained in a piece of plastic about the size of his hand, to Tuffy's harness. At first Tuffy didn't appear to mind the suction cups on either side of his body just behind the flippers or the "tweet, tweet" tone the device sounded with each heartbeat. He took a few smelts from Wally and made a circuit of the pool in an apparently normal manner. But then we knew something was wrong because the dolphin went into one of his pouts. He swam to the far side of the pool, placed his head against the wall, and stayed there, occasionally bobbing his head, clapping his jaws, and making odd low-intensity squeals and gurgling sounds.

This pouting behavior never lasted for more than five minutes. Tuffy pouted when asked to do something he did not want to do, when confused about what to do, or when there was a difference of opinion between Tuffy and his trainer about Tuffy's performance. The dolphin always turned directly away from the trainer and swam as far away as possible. I wondered what would happen if Tuffy chose to pout in the open sea.

Now we watched the most striking feature of Tuffy's pouts: They always ended abruptly. Wally and I saw the dolphin's body relax and his posture change. The smoldering rage vanished, and he came scooting across the surface toward us, gray face smiling broadly.

For an hour we recorded the dolphin's heartbeat as he swam around the pool. Later we hoped to compare this data with data from dives Tuffy would make at sea wearing the same device. After I removed the heartbeat device, we left Tuffy to rest until after lunch, when we had arranged for boats and people to move the dolphin to his ocean pen.

In preparation for the move Mo had taken Tuffy's portable pen apart, toted it up to the long sandy beach by Mugu Pier, reassembled it, and floated it out to anchor in about sixty feet of water, about two hundred yards from shore. To tow the pen out, Mo used an amphibious vehicle called a DUWK, borrowed from the Seabee detachment at Point Mugu. The DUWK could roll along like a truck on land, then drive into the water and become a boat by shifting gears to power a propeller. A compromise, neither a good truck nor a good boat, the DUWK could be used only in fairly calm seas.

We did not have a harbor at Point Mugu. Besides the DUWK, which we could borrow only occasionally, there were two other means for getting out to the ocean, and both were dependent on good weather. We could use a winch on the end of Mugu Pier to lower a small boat into the water, or we could run through the lagoon mouth in one of our small boats. An experienced driver could navigate the lagoon mouth even when the water was a little rough, but it was risky, as we would learn.

At 1:30 P.M. everything was ready, but now Tuffy refused to get into the lifting sling. Wally called with the strobe, and Tuffy raced over to collect a fish, then raced away, ignoring Wally's signal to enter the sling. After a dozen repetitions of this errant behavior, the trainer grew impatient. "Darn you old tough rascal," growled Wally. "People waiting, boats waiting, and you decide to be contrary."

Wally decided to play an ace and use coercion, something he seldom did in training animals. Tuffy had been caught and taken from the Gulf of Mexico in a net, so Wally threw a net into the pool. Although it never touched Tuffy, the net had an immediate effect. Tuffy returned to Wally's call and remained next to him, absolutely still, as the sling was put in the water again. Promptly on Wally's signal, the dolphin swam into the canvas.

Wally and a sailor got into a boat at the end of the

pier. Mo, Marty, and two of the sailors carried Tuffy in his sling, wearing the harness and leash, into the mild surf that lapped at the white sand. When Wally came up in the outboard, Mo threw him the end of Tuffy's fifty-foot leash. Then Mo and Marty led the dolphin out to shoulder-deep water and released him.

Marty dove under a swell and in a few quick strokes got back to the beach. Mo paused, and Tuffy refused to swim away, staying close beside him, keeping body contact with his head and flipper. Mo patted Tuffy's head, then pushed the dolphin out toward Wally, who was waiting fifty feet away at the end of the leash. But Tuffy came back. When Mo pushed the dolphin toward the boat again and turned to wade ashore, the dolphin seemed to panic. Tuffy rushed forward, ramming Mo with enough force to knock him down in the waist-deep water. When Mo reached out to push the dolphin away again, Tuffy bit his hand.

The bite seemed to be less an attack than an attempt to hold on. Wally gripped the leash and gunned the engine, pulling the dolphin seaward. As Mo waded out, blood dripping from his hand, a struggle ensued between Wally and Tuffy. Wally's boat towed the dolphin seaward while Tuffy tried frantically to swim toward Mo on shore. The force of the tow on the dolphin's harness overwhelmed his swimming and stood him upright. As Tuffy bobbed backward through the swells, he looked toward us, squealing. The scene was simultaneously amusing and heartrending. From all appearances the dolphin thought we were abandoning him.

Gradually, Wally coaxed his reluctant pupil up to the boat. The dolphin seemed to recognize a familiar face or situation, for he turned suddenly and followed the craft as he had learned to do in the lagoon. Wally tied up to the floating ocean pen, opened the gate, and dangled the strobe inside. Tuffy swam in, and Wally allowed him a few minutes to explore the familiar surroundings of his pen. Then he exercised the dolphin around it, having him swim in and out the gate. Tuffy now behaved normally, following the boat to the pier and back. Satisfied that Tuffy's panic had subsided, Wally removed the harness and left the dolphin for his first night in his new home.

Tuffy's main task now would be retrieving a weighted ring attached to a buoy and a length of line. We planned to test Tuffy's maximum diving depth by gradually lengthening the line between the buoy and the ring. At the time dolphins were not thought to be deep divers. In the scientific literature I had read, the weight of opinion seemed to be that dolphins stayed mostly in the upper one hundred feet of the ocean. Their maximum diving depth often was said to be one hundred or two hundred feet. One French researcher had found deep-water fish in the stomachs of bottle-nosed dolphins killed off Africa, but no diving experiments had been done with dolphins in the open sea.

During some of the dives we hoped to have Tuffy wear the telemetry device on his harness. Seals that had been force-dived in the laboratory had shown a striking reduction in heart rate. The rate often fell from more than one hundred beats per minute to ten per minute or lower. This response had become known as "diving bradycardia" and was the central feature among a series of physiological responses that had become known as the "diving reflex." But most of this work had been done with laboratory animals, and I wanted to find out whether Tuffy's heart responded in this way when the dolphin was diving freely in the ocean.

On the first day Wally had worked only in the ocean pen, but the following day he harnessed Tuffy and called him through the gate into the open. The dolphin swam beside the boat, never roving even to the end of the leash. After running a short distance, Wally cut the engine and allowed the boat to drift. Wally dropped a fish to the dolphin and threw out the ring with only ten feet of line. Tuffy retrieved it immediately. Wally kept throwing out the ring and buoy, gradually increasing the length of line. After the dolphin made five good trips to forty feet, the maximum depth Tuffy had dived in the lagoon, Wally decided to call it a perfect day and headed back to the pen. On the return trip Tuffy never strayed from Wally's side.

The following morning seas had come up and the water was too rough to launch the workboat from the pier. It was after noon, and the ocean was still gray and bleak, when Wally and Marty drove a boat out through the lagoon mouth. The trip was a little bouncy, but Tuffy seemed glad to see them. Driving the boat a quarter of a mile seaward, Marty and Wally had Tuffy make numerous dives, the deepest to eighty-five feet.

The next morning large waves were breaking on shore. Gates and I motored with Wally through the lagoon mouth. We climbed high over the first big wave, and in the following trough we angled north toward Tuffy in his ocean pen. As we passed some surfers clad in wet suits on another swell, I saw Tuffy's pen in the distance, black like a floating log, on a gray ocean under a gray sky. The timbers shifted disjointedly as each wave passed, one corner rising, the other falling to let the mass of water by. The enclosure drew strength from this flexibility.

As we approached, Tuffy poked his head above a swell and stood upright in the water, dancing on his flukes higher and higher to gain a better view of us. The dolphin squealed and shook a smiling head as Wally leaped from our small boat onto the corner of the heaving structure and secured the boat with a line. I marveled at how motionless Tuffy remained in the swells. As Wally put the harness on the dolphin, Tuffy rose and fell on the surface exactly in unison with the oil-drum float where Wally sat. Compared to the dolphin's grace in the sea, any man seems out of place there, but Wally seemed especially incongruous in rubber coveralls with suspenders over his shoulders and a straw hat on his head. The trainer would have seemed in place tromping around a Missouri barnyard but not here straddling timbers in the Pacific. Yet he negotiated the heaving framework of the pen and harnessed Tuffy with ease as the waves rose and fell around us. I could not have done half so well.

As we sliced through the crests of waves toward the practice area, Tuffy surfed beside our boat. A dolphin learns to surf only minutes after birth. The little calf stays close to its mother, just to one side of her dorsal fin, and the movement of her large body through the water sets up a pressure wave where the offspring rides. As they grow, dolphins perfect their surfing skills. Dolphins will ride the pressure wave set up by boats or by large whales passing through the water, and as Tuffy taught us, dolphins often will generate their own waves in tanks and literally surf against the pool wall. At the stern of our outboard boat the push of the engine's propeller generated a wave, and Tuffy quickly found it. Tuffy's stern wave surfing allowed us to move along faster, since the dolphin, carried along by our power, would not be tired out by his run to the dive station.

We cut the engine and let the boat drift. Wally called Tuffy forward, gave him a smelt for poking the strobe, and removed the leash. I threw out the ring with fifty feet of line, and the dolphin dove straight down. Based on his performance yesterday, Tuffy should have been back in sixty seconds or less, but to our consternation, the dolphin vanished.

If time were measured in anguish and worry, I would have said we were there for an hour searching each wave for Tuffy. By my watch, however, it was only four minutes before we saw him, perched on the down side of a wave coming just past our bow, flukes hardly moving. Effortlessly, he rolled to one side, eyeing us as the wave he rode went past us. About three minutes passed before he suddenly appeared behind our boat again. He paused to sucker a fish from Wally by touching the strobe, then sped away to catch another wave. Like spectators to an earthquake, we clung to our rocking boat to watch the dolphin's play. He continued for almost an hour. We were awed by his surfing display yet uneasy about its outcome. When Tuffy finally answered Wally's call, he made retrievals as deep as 110 feet. On the last two dives Tuffy went seaward to catch a wave, and as he reached our buoy, he let the wave catapult his body toward the depths.

As the offshore wind got stronger, the waves grew. "Let's go home," said Wally. Quickly agreeing, I was relieved when Wally snapped the leash on Tuffy's harness. When the dolphin was back in his ocean pen, we fed Tuffy what remained of his fifteen pounds of fish. He deserved a good meal. He had shown us how dolphins use the natural force of a wave to hurl them toward the depths. He had done this while completely free of any physical control from us. And more important, he had chosen to come back with us to enter his floating pen.

In the succeeding week Tuffy's dives reached two hundred feet, but we encountered a problem with the buoy, line, and weighted ring. Sometimes the trailing line got tangled around Tuffy's tail or snarled in the dolphin's harness as he was bringing the ring back to the surface. To solve this problem we devised a new method, using a switch and a buzzer in an old automobile steering wheel mounted at the end of three hundred feet of electrical cable. At the opposite end of the cable we installed a control box with a switch the trainer could activate. When this switch was thrown, the buzzer sounded in the wheel. The dolphin would be trained to dive at the sound of the buzzer and press the wheel with his snout, tilting it to actuate a second switch to turn off the sound. Tuffy could return to the surface without a trailing line to contend with, and we could more accurately time how long it took Tuffy to go down and return to the surface.

While we built this new device, Wally began having Tuffy practice with divers in the ocean. Marty and another diver went to eighty-five feet, each diver carrying a strobe and a plastic bag full of fish. The plan was that the first diver wuld call Tuffy and give him a fish for touching the strobe; then the other diver, twenty or thirty feet away, would call the dolphin. By calling the dolphin back and forth between the divers, we hoped to keep Tuffy underwater for as long as he would stay. We could record his heartbeat with the telemetry device, and we might get more information about how long the dolphin could hold his breath.

Wally called Tuffy from the pen and led him over to the area where the divers waited on the bottom. The dolphin lay on the surface, snout pointed downward, scanning the depths below. It appeared to me that he knew exactly where the divers were. When the trainer took off the leash, the dolphin shot down immediately, even before the divers called him. Fourteen fathoms down, Marty felt a jarring poke on his shoulder. Startled, he turned to see a large dolphin eye in the middle of the view from his faceplate. When Marty pushed the dolphin away, Tuffy swam to the second diver. Marty flicked on his strobe, and the dolphin made a leisurely circle just above the second diver's head, then coasted toward the flashing strobe in Marty's hand. Tuffy touched the strobe, and Marty pulled a fish from his bag to feed the dolphin. The second diver turned on his strobe, repeating the procedure. The flashing lights and the juicy crumbs from Tuffy's food attracted swimming fish like swarms of insects around a summer lantern. The dolphin stayed with the divers for about two minutes, then answered Wally's call back to the surface; he took a fish from the trainer and almost immediately dived again. The dolphin showed no reluctance to stay with the divers for four minutes, slowly cruising back and forth between them. With swarms of live fish swimming about him, Tuffy never detoured from the divers.

In March, rough weather complicated the task of bringing Tuffy back through the entrance to the lagoon. During calm seas and especially at high tide the dolphin easily followed the boat, but in rough seas there were problems. Wally had lengthened the leash to 150 feet to give the dolphin plenty of room, and often the keepers could race ahead with the boat, then lead Tuffy in after them. Sometimes we could leave Tuffy in the ocean, just outside the lagoon entrance, catch the proper wave to get our boat inside, then simply call Tuffy in with the strobe. This was beautiful when it worked. But sometimes Tuffy did not want to go in. In one instance we had to go back to the ocean, where we found the dolphin hanging around his ocean pen. Wally decided to put him back in the pen rather than risk another loss of contact with him at the lagoon entrance. "If it's rough tomorrow, we'll leave him in the pen and fast him," said Wally. "He didn't work well today. He may work a lot better when he's hungry."

The following morning the sea looked angry. I would not risk winching the dolphin onto the DUWK in such rough water. For a while Wally and I watched his pupil from the end of Mugu Pier. Tuffy seemed happy, almost as if relaxing. The dolphin lay on his back, playing with a strand of golden-brown kelp draped across his belly. Occasionally, he tugged at the strand with his mouth and lifted it on flukes or flipper.

"Small-craft warnings from Point Conception to the Mexican border," reported the radio announcer as I drove to work the next day. Offshore winds had increased during the night. I arrived at our Point Mugu dolphin facility facing an inhospitable ocean. "We can't take the DUWK out today. Small-craft warnings, throughout southern California," said the Seabee dispatcher when I called.

We had not expected a storm. We had fasted Tuffy

yesterday with hopes that he would work better today. Now it looked as if we could not get out to the pen to feed the dolphin, much less to work with him at sea. Wally and I sat on the sand, looking out at the big waves rolling in and crashing onto the beach between us and Tuffy's pen. Through binoculars we occasionally could see the dolphin's head rise above the water as a wave rolled past.

"The waves are big but slow and smooth," said Wally. "Maybe we could take the Boston Whaler out through the lagoon mouth." It seemed worth a try. Gates volunteered to drive the small, open boat. He had the most experience in running the Whaler from lagoon to ocean, and his surfer's skill in judging the waves was a great asset. We sped up the lagoon in the sixteen-foot outboard toward the opening to the sea. Gates and I were comfortably insulated by our wet suits; Wally wore his usual well-worn denim coveralls. A metal whistle dangled from a chain around his neck. In one hand he held a bucket containing Tuffy's eighteen pounds of fish; with his other hand he held onto the gunnel of the boat. As we rounded the sandbar into the lagoon mouth, I felt troubled. From the beach the waves had appeared large. From our new perspective they were gigantic.

We had to time our approach to the ocean just right. Our boat must arrive at the lagoon entrance just as a wave crashed and flattened out into a frothy white boil. At full speed we would try to reach the next wave in deeper water before it crested and curled over. Gates cut the outboard to idle. I felt my heart pounding. We waited in the shallow, calm water of the lagoon, watching the huge waves crash just ahead until we had decided the largest waves were coming in threes. Gates gunned the engine as a third giant started to curl and fall. We sped forward, smashing through the broad boil in perfect time, then raced across the trough straight for the next wave.

Exhilaration. We were lifted smoothly so high that I could see my laboratory three hundred yards away across the tall dunes. But the exhilaration was short-lived as gravity forced me to look down and our easy lift turned into a roller-coaster dive. As the propeller broke the surface, the muffled sound of the engine changed pitch to a rough squeal. The bow hit, then cold green water was all around us.

Irresistible force drove me underwater into the sandy bottom. I didn't know which way was up. Luckily, my head broke the surface. Feet planted in the sand, I stood in the area of white water we had powered through a moment earlier. Then, with a giant slap on the back, the bow of the boat knocked me face down into the sand. I felt the smooth fiberglass hull slide over the thick neoprene on my back. I got to my knees and gasped for air as seawater splashed over me. I could see Gates waist-deep in the water, coming toward me. As the boat swung around, I saw four white knuckles over the silvery steel bar that ran around the Whaler's gunnel. I struggled to my feet and helped Gates push the boat into the lagoon toward calm waters. Wally crouched in the boat, holding the gunnel with one hand and his soaked straw hat with the other. The whistle hung from Wally's neck, dripping seawater. The bucket and Tuffy's fish were gone.

No one spoke as we dragged the Whaler onto a sandy beach inside the lagoon, but I felt a consensus that this would be our last attempt to get food to Tuffy today. I joined Mo on the beach at 4:30 P.M. for a last look. "Do you think your pen will hold up?" I asked, as he peered through binoculars.

"It's held up good so far, hasn't it?" he snapped, sitting down on the sand. "Filling with kelp, though. That could put a lot of weight on the net and maybe break the wood." He handed me the glasses. "If it breaks up, there's nothing we can do about it. Tuffy can swim a lot better than we can."

"I've discussed it with Woody and Wally," I said. "We all think the biggest problem is to get some food to the dolphin. If he gets too hungry, he might jump out and go foraging on his own. We need to keep up his confidence in us as a source of food."

"What will you try next?" asked Mo.

"Woody called surface craft," I replied. "They said no dice because of weather, but Marty talked to the chief boatswain's mate, Boots Johnson, and Boots said he would talk to the C.O. about letting him take us out in one of the 85-footers tomorrow morning. They're the same boats the Coast Guard uses. I know they can take rough water."

"But you can't tie off to the pen with the 85-footer," Mo noted. "That big boat might bash the pen to pieces before you could get the dolphin fed."

"I think it's worth a try," I said. "Maybe we can get enough fish in by making a few runs past the pen. Anyway, we can't use the DUWK in these waves, and we crashed trying to get out through the lagoon mouth in the Whaler today."

"It's a lucky thing you didn't drown somebody," said Mo. "Wally can't swim a lick."

"What do you mean Wally can't swim?" I replied incredulously.

"That's what I said. Wally can't swim. He nearly

drowned once in the big pool down at the park. Sinks just like a chimpanzee."

"Like a chimp?"

"They can't swim either. Too much muscle and bone. One of them fell in once, sank like a rock to the bottom, same as Wally. I pulled the chimp out, darn near got my arm chewed off."

The news was frightening. To think of how many times I had been to sea with Wally, and I had had no idea he couldn't swim. A vivid image of his white knuckles clutching the gunnel flashed through my mind.

The next morning the whitecaps on the ocean were not as prominent, but the waves were still large. Marty and I boarded the 85-footer *Ten Boat,* wearing our wet suits and carrying a bucket of fish. I noticed above the wheel house a neatly printed sign: A COLLISION AT SEA CAN SPOIL YOUR WHOLE DAY.

As our craft bucked the first waves past the breakwater of Port Hueneme harbor, a heavy mist rolled in from the sea. Boots Johnson turned the boat south down the coast, cutting obliquely across deep troughs. The sky closed in on us; supported by angry water, we rocked with each passing swell. Water spilled over the bow when we bumped hard into a wave, but there was little doubt that Boots and *Ten Boat* could take us to Tuffy's pen.

But today not only weather, but fate as well, seemed to be against us. "Malfunctioning radar," Boots reported. When he called back to get some technical advice about fixing it, he received a peremptory order to return to port. I guess the C.O. reckoned it was too risky having one of his boats out in such rough water without radar. I'm sure that running through his mind were the possible words of a military court prosecutor:

"And you say *Ten Boat* was lost in heavy seas on a mission to feed a porpoise?"

As we passed Point Mugu's main runway on the way back to the lab, the rain abated, and incredibly, the sun started to burn through the fog. A bright orange navy helicopter taxied toward us, stirring up water pooled at the end of the runway. "Helicopter!" I gasped. "We can feed Tuffy from a helicopter."

A friend of mine flew helicopters, so I called him right away. "Sure," he said. "Come on down. Surface operations have been canceled for three days, and we've had nothing to do. I need practice."

I arrived at the helicopter pad in ten minutes, still in my wet suit, holding Tuffy's fish bucket in hand. A crewman outfitted me with a survival vest, put a hard, plastic helmet on my head, and plugged me into a microphone so I could talk to the pilot.

We lifted off the runway in bright sunshine and made a wide circle over the Pacific, then turned south along the shore toward the ocean pier where Woody, Mo, and Wally were standing to watch the operation. Examining Tuffy's pen as the chopper descended from an elevation of about two hundred feet, I saw that it was almost full of kelp. One corner was submerged, another awash with a heavy burden of the golden-brown strands. I could not see space enough for the dolphin. With a sinking heart I concluded that Tuffy was gone.

We could not blame Tuffy for leaving. He had not been fed in three days, and the framework of the kelp-filled pen appeared to be sinking. "I can't see the dolphin," said the pilot as we circled the pen. The crewman latched a safety line around my waist so that I could lean out the open side door of the helicopter, about fifty feet above the pen. Peering down, I searched every corner of the pen. Finally I made out a gray form, deep in one corner. It was the only space in the pen not covered by kelp. This must be the dolphin, but I could see no movement in the form. Could Tuffy have become entangled in netting and kelp and drowned?

I threw a large mackerel as hard as I could at the gray form. The wind and prop wash sent the silvery blue fish spiraling outside the pen, but the effect of its splash was immediate: The dolphin started, then turned and looked toward the splash. Tuffy was alive! I felt a rush of exhilaration and gratitude. I threw another mackerel, this time accounting for the wind. A direct hit, right in Tuffy's corner. The dolphin grabbed the fish instantly, and I threw another.

Tuffy looked up toward me while the third fish fell. When the fourth fish arrived, Tuffy intercepted it in the air. The dolphin peered at me, moving his flukes to keep his forebody above the water; his open mouth reminded me of an expectant puppy. I sat in the open door of the chopper with the fish bucket beside me and pitched down fish after fish.

Now and then my aim was bad and the fish went astray. That pained me, and I suspect it caused the hungry dolphin temporary anguish, but Tuffy kept his eye on the funny, noisy bird that hovered overhead. I imagine the dolphin was squealing and whistling with glee, but in the heavy aviator's helmet and earphones, I could not hear a single sound outside the helicopter. I felt strangely detached and unreal. The stormy waves below, the pen surging in the current, and the excited dolphin all seemed like the frames of a silent movie passing before my eyes. I wondered whether Tuffy might also have strange feelings. Oh, I thought, if only I could know what this dolphin from the Gulf of Mexico thought about these strange events in the Pacific and the strange habits and contraptions of the men who tended him.

During that feeding by helicopter Tuffy ate almost fifteen pounds of mackerel plus his vitamins. As for me, my peace of mind was restored because my friend from the sea was still with us. Like a giant mosquito, the helicopter flitted back to the Point Mugu runway. I thanked the crew profusely and returned the heavy helmet and survival gear.

The sun was warm the next noon when we drove the DUWK across the beach and out to Tuffy's pen to bring the dolphin ashore and to study damage from the storm and kelp. (Giant California kelp, *Macrocystis pyrifera*, is one of the world's larger plants; it reaches lengths of two hundred feet and grows at a rate of up to two feet per day. The kelp bed is an underwater forest where a whole ecosystem thrives.) We lifted the dolphin out of the water and headed toward shore, where many more tons of brown, rotting algae lay on the beach in piles like unkempt stacks of hay. With a day's warm sun, the stacks had settled into mushy piles containing fibrous kelp strands, flies, maggots, and dark goo. That kelp had caused us many problems over the past few days, and it wasn't through with me yet. As the DUWK lurched onto the beach with Tuffy swinging securely in his sling, I lost my balance and fell headlong into one of the stinky piles.

It did not take Wally long to teach Tuffy to use the wheel and buzzer we had designed to replace the weighted ring in deep-diving tests. We had tested the system along the road in front of our facility. Three hundred feet of cable connected the wheel to a control box. Wally flicked a toggle on the control box, a red light flashed, and we heard the faint buzzing from the wheel. Wally walked down the road and tilted the wheel. The buzzing quit, and I saw the red light on the control box go off, and a yellow light came on. Wally walked back. "Three hundred feet," he said. "That's as long as a football field. To dive that deep, Tuffy will be like a football player running from one goal to the other and back again holding his breath the whole time."

In early May we returned the dolphin to his offshore pen. The day was sunny, and the ocean was clear. We gave Tuffy an hour to get reacquainted with his pen. Mo had cleaned out the kelp and mended several holes in the netting.

The beautiful jellyfish *Pelagia,* known to some as medusae, dotted the water. Large medusae remind me of decorated beach balls cut in half. Maroon stripes run down from a ring that encircles the dome, and the skin between the stripes often has a pinkish tint. Under the colored mantle hang long tentacles that can cause painful stings.

Wally released Tuffy from the pen, and we headed seaward with the dolphin beside our stern. Soon Tuffy had turned back, and as Wally slowed the boat to put in the strobe, I noticed a large medusa floating near our boat. Rather than coming to the strobe, Tuffy went over and poked his snout under the medusa's colorful mantle, lifting the jellyfish well out of the water. By treading water with his powerful flukes and leaning backward, the dolphin let the medusa slide slowly down his belly into the water. We watched with trepidation.

"Doesn't he know that thing can sting?" Wally said. He slapped the water and put the strobe in again to lure Tuffy back to the boat and away from danger. The dolphin would have none of it. Within twenty feet of the boat, right before our eyes, Tuffy insisted on having his frolic with this poisonous creature.

The dolphin has bad skin already! I thought in exasperation. What if he is severely stung? What if he breaks out in blisters? What medication do I have to treat a dolphin with a jellyfish sting?

Tuffy continued his revelry with the slippery mass of jellyfish, coming up underneath it, rolling along so that every inch of his body from the tip of his snout to the end of his tail touched the medusa. The dolphin then dived under in a cartwheeling motion and holding his mouth open wide, brought the medusa up with maroon-striped mantle bulging from both sides of his jaws. Tuffy seemed to savor the whole mass for a moment, then chopped it in half with one quick motion. He let the jelly slide slowly out the corners of his mouth as he leaned backward, eyes closed. Tuffy continued to amuse himself for about twenty minutes, destroying three more medusae and damaging several others. Finally, when he tired of this play, he answered Wally's call and we continued on to the diving site. I could only surmise that Tuffy got enjoyable sensations from such intimate contact with the jellyfish. This thing that stings and irritates our skin apparently gave pleasure to him. I observed the dolphin closely, but I saw no sign that contact with the medusae had done him any harm.

During the test Tuffy made ten dives in clear Pacific

water perhaps a half-mile seaward of his pen. The new system worked well, and Tuffy went down to 150 feet. The progress was slow, but watching the dolphin dive was thrilling. Tuffy lay at the surface, his eye seemingly welded to Wally. When the trainer turned on the buzzer, Tuffy blew. His chest contracted and immediately expanded again as he took in air for the trip downward. With no waves to catapult him, the dolphin simply turned downward, his flukes extending out of the water like the feet of a man doing a handstand. Tuffy went straight down the wire. With my free hand I raised a clipboard to make a shady spot on the water, creating a window through the mirrorlike surface.

Tuffy's flukes moved slowly at first, as if pushing against a heavy load. But with each beat of his tail, the dolphin seemed to gain momentum and speed. The flukes pumped faster as my view of the dolphin grew fainter, the image fading into the smoky blue depths. Tuffy didn't tarry below at the wheel. He reappeared in only a few seconds, materializing from the abyss like a tiny cloud against a blue Pacific horizon. When he returned from the depths I always watched for his eyes. He cocked his head back in such a way that the dark orbs on either side of his head were clearly visible to me. Both eyes seemed to be focused upward on the same shadow-window through which I peered down. I was fascinated by the dolphin's gaze. If only I could hold up another clipboard for a window on Tuffy's mind, to see his thoughts as clearly as I viewed his form through the water's surface.

Tuffy coasted the last few feet to the surface, touched the strobe, took a fish from Wally's hand and swallowed it, and only then drew a deep breath. His breath-holding control amazed me. I remember snorkeling down to 40 feet one time. On my way back to the surface my lungs burned; looking up, my whole being focused on the shimmering silver of the surface. Reaching the air, I lay on the surface gasping for a moment. When Tuffy surfaced after his deep dive, his first breath seemed almost incidental. I judged that Tuffy's dive to 150 feet taxed him about as much as my diving to 10.

Some of what is written about dolphin diving is all wrong, I mused as we returned to the pen with Tuffy surfing on our stern wave. Marine mammals are supposed to dive after exhaling most of the air from their lungs, which is one way of avoiding the bends. Seals have been observed to snort out air as they submerge. But Tuffy took a deep breath and dived. He seemed to use the air in his lungs for buoyancy, to give him a little extra help in coming back to the surface. As any child who has sat on a balloon knows, air is compressible. By thirty-three feet, as the dolphin descended, the volume of air in his lungs compressed by half. Thus Tuffy actually got less buoyant as he dove, and he gained speed. The air remaining in the dolphin's lungs expanded during the trip back up, making Tuffy more buoyant as he approached the surface and helping him to coast the last few feet.

During May and early June we continued to test Tuffy's diving as far as a mile out to sea. Tuffy had been so reliable at answering the strobe that Wally quit using the leash. After harnessing the dolphin, Wally would open the pen gate and dangle the strobe in the water outside, and Tuffy would shoot through the gate, eager to go to work.

Tuffy had seemed to enjoy the presence of divers

who had filmed his performance in the sonar demonstration, and now that he was working reliably in the open ocean, we asked the frogmen to join us more often. Marty, in charge of our diving work, told me that Tuffy usually went out of his way to approach divers from the rear. Sometimes the diver would feel a tap, occasionally a very hard tap, on his shoulder and turn to see a large eye in the middle of his faceplate.

By calling the dolphin back and forth between them, two divers could keep the dolphin underwater for almost five minutes while I sat in a boat above with a hydrophone recording the beep, beep, beep of Tuffy's heart signal. The heartbeat data were surprising. We had come to expect that the dolphin would show a pronounced diving bradycardia, like the drastic reduction in heart rate observed in seals and other marine animals underwater. But Tuffy's heartbeat during dives slowed only moderately.

I learned that dolphins usually have a two-speed heart, which beats faster when the dolphin is breathing and slower between breaths. During the dives the dolphin's heart beat 60 to 90 times a minute, but on the surface after a breath the rate increased to a range of 100 to 150 beats per minute. When the animal was resting out of the water on a rubber pad, the heart rate was 30 or 40 per minute between breaths, increasing to 70 or 80 with the blow. The two-speed heart rhythm was one of the interesting physiological adjusments these mammals have made to live underwater.

One Friday a heavy fog hung over the shore as Wally, Marty, and I went through the lagoon mouth in our new Boston Whaler and headed toward Tuffy's pen. We planned to bring him back to the lagoon at the end of the day's tests. As usual Tuffy seemed eager to join us. We plowed through the fog, taking a bearing by dead reckoning to a deep-water spot about a mile from the pen. Occasionally, Wally dropped a fish to the dolphin; Tuffy raced forward briefly to snag the fish before settling back into his wave just to the left of our big outboard engine. In the gray fog I could see perhaps one hundred feet in all directions.

We stopped at a point we judged to be over deep water and let out some cable. Wally liked to start the dolphin with a shallow dive, then move deeper and deeper. As the fog slowly dissipated and the sun broke through, Tuffy dived to 175 feet. Then the wheel hit bottom.

By the time we had reeled in the cable, moved farther seaward, and put the wheel back down, all that remained of the morning fog was a haze that cloaked the eastern mountains and the horizon. Although the weather was better, Tuffy now refused to dive. He played with a medusa for a while and at one point appeared to be chasing a shoal of small fish that jumped at the surface only fifty feet from our boat. When Wally called Tuffy with the strobe, the dolphin came over and took the thawed fish that Wally offered.

"Let's go home," said Wally. "He won't dive anymore today."

Marty started the engine and turned the boat toward the low, black form of Mugu Pier, a mile in the distance. We were about halfway back when we realized that Tuffy had disappeared from the stern wave. Marty cut the engine. A breeze had come up, and there was an occasional whitecap. We stood in the silence, staring across the sea, examining each tongue of white foam. Back to back we looked, each searching a third of the sea around us, each occasionally squinting at the other guy's territory in case he was missing something.

Wally put the strobe in several times and took it out again each time after giving the dolphin a couple of minutes to respond. Marty started the engine, and we headed back toward the dive site. A quarter of a mile farther on, we stopped again to call Tuffy. Again we strained our eyes against the whitecaps and the glare. We could see an orange helicopter hovering in the distance, and farther seaward an 85-footer steamed north, leaving in its wake smoke and white water.

Then I saw something in the water, maybe two hundred yards off. We gunned it over there, but it was not the dolphin. Floating on the surface, low in the water like a half-submerged oil drum, an elephant seal was "bottling," lying on the surface sound asleep. Just as we arrived, the three-thousand-pound male seal started, snorted through his great proboscis, and sank straight down. I could see his two wide eyes down below. The elephant seal backed away, keeping suspicious eyes on us. We never saw him again.

We went on calling Tuffy but got no response. Growing anxious now, we set up a more methodical search pattern. We explored a square mile of sea surface by going as close as we could estimate to the last dive site, then to the lagoon mouth, then to Tuffy's pen, and finally out to sea again. There was no sign of the dolphin. The search continued as our faces reddened in the sun and our eyes burned in the glare. We repeated the pattern, working to the center of the square, until Marty announced that we were nearly out of fuel. "Drop me off at the pen," said Wally. "I'll keep calling him from there while you two go back to the facility and get the gas."

By the time Marty and I returned to sea an hour later, it was mid-afternoon. We brought drinking water, jackets, hamburgers, and an extra tank of gasoline. The ocean was full of whitecaps. After we crossed the breakers at the lagoon mouth and turned north toward the pen, I saw Wally's straw hat, bright white against the blue ocean. He was not staring seaward as we had left him but looking down at the water. His hands seemed to be occupied. There was Tuffy, lying at the surface with his belly up, getting a rubdown.

"He appeared out of the chop about twenty minutes after you left," said Wally. "He swam up, taking his time as if nothing unusual had ever happened. He came through the gate, touched the strobe, poked his nose through the bars of my pulpit, and has been lying here like this ever since."

A few days later I discovered the full story of our search for errant Tuffy when by chance I saw my friend the helicopter pilot. "Hey, Sam, what were you guys doing last Friday just off the mouth of Mugu Lagoon?" asked the pilot.

"We were trying to do some diving experiments," I replied.

"It sure was interesting to me," said the pilot. "I must have spent an hour over that area on Friday waiting for drone pickups. It was interesting to watch you and your porpoise. He would stay exactly the same distance behind you, maybe about three hundred yards. Every time you changed course, he would change course. When your boat would turn and go toward the porpoise, he would swim a few hundred yards seaward and then fall in behind you again as the boat went by. How on earth did you train him to do that?"

I was too embarrassed to tell my friend the truth.

Instead I told him about dolphin training and diving and how we had taught Tuffy to follow boats at sea. I just neglected to say how closely we meant to have the animal follow.

After this experience we developed a more relaxed attitude about Tuffy's occasional straying. The dolphin developed a habit of laying back when we left the dive site to return to the pen. We would drive along for a distance with the dolphin in his customary position by the stern of the boat, then suddenly we would notice he was gone. Because it seemed to Wally that the animal had come up with a strategy to keep the people around as long as possible, he designed a counterstrategy of varying the time when we left for the day. Sometimes Wally would stay at the pen and play with the dolphin for a while after the session. Other times Wally would stop in the middle of a session, go back to the pen, take off Tuffy's harness, rub the animal down, put the harness back on, and then return to the dive site. Working with Tuffy in the open sea kept the trainer on his toes; Wally tried to keep Tuffy guessing as well.

Two of the great triumphs of modern medicine—the production of vaccines against killer diseases and the discovery of antibiotics to combat diease-causing microorganisms—were already part of my repertoire. I had learned to use antibiotics in dolphins, accounting for their differences in metabolism and kidney function and adjusting dosages and schedules accordingly. I also could vaccinate the animals against their most common deadly disease, erysipelas. But a third great triumph of medical science, anesthesia for major surgery, was still not possible. Dolphins stopped breathing when under anesthesia, and I thought their two-speed heart might have something to do with it.

No matter how original the research or how specialized the field of science, the researcher soon becomes aware of predecessors who thought the same thoughts and planned similar schemes. Earlier in this century Dr. Orthello Langworthy tried to anesthetize a dolphin with ether out on the blowing beach sand of

North Carolina, not far from where the Wright brothers first achieved motorized flight. Langworthy wrote about his experiences with dolphins in several papers. He recognized the challenge of studying their physiology and their great brain. He knew that anesthesia was essential for pursuing such studies in a humane manner. Unfortunately, Langworthy's dolphin died under the ether.

Where Langworthy had failed, I hoped to succeed. Although aviation had made great strides after Kitty Hawk, a half-century had passed and dolphin anesthesia was still not practical. Like Langworthy, I knew that anesthesia would help us in experiments needed for understanding the whales' physiology and mysterious brain.

Characteristically, Woody cautioned me that the task of devising a safe anesthetic procedure for dolphins would not be easy. He reminded me that he had been curator of Marineland of Florida in 1955 at the time of the so-called "Johns Hopkins Expedition." Three distinguished neuroscientists from Johns Hopkins University had come to Marineland to map the dolphin cortex, to determine which parts of the brain surface responded to sounds, light flashes, and pressure on the skin. Studies of these and other such sensory stimuli would reveal a great deal about the workings of the dolphin's large brain. But to expose the surface of the brain required major surgery, and the scientists failed to foresee the difficulty of anesthetizing dolphins.

The problem, Woody explained, was that bottlenosed dolphins, and apparently all whales, do not breathe as land mammals do. Instead of inhaling and exhaling every few seconds in a rhythmic fashion, dolphins have adjusted their breathing pattern to life in the water; they breathe in a fraction of a second, then hold the air in their lungs for fifteen to sixty seconds before breathing again. Before surgically examining the first dolphin's brain, the Johns Hopkins group anesthetized the dolphin with a shot of barbiturate. The animal relaxed, lost the air in its lungs, and never breathed again. In their subsequent attempts to map the brain, the neurosurgeons used a simple respirator to keep the animal breathing while it was anesthetized, but the machine proved inadequate. After several more animals died, the experimenters abandoned the surgical approach as a means of studying the dolphin brain.

A breakthrough that would permit me to devise an anesthesia method for sick animals came with the development of a control device by Dr. Forrest Bird, inventor of the Bird respirator. The control device allowed the respirator to mimic the normal dolphin respiratory pattern: inflating the lungs, holding them inflated for twenty or thirty seconds, then rapidly deflating and inflating them again.

We were able to get this new Bird respirator and other necessary equipment, and Woody agreed that I should test my own ideas for surgical anesthesia on dolphins. I did not want to use Tuffy as a guinea pig, and none of the trainers at Point Mugu wanted me to practice on any of their dolphins, so the only available subjects were the two Lags that Mo had caught.

As a first step in our project Ensign Frank Harvey and I went to Palm Springs, California, where Dr. Bird and his associates instructed us in the operation of the new machine. A group in Miami led by Drs. Eugene Nagel and Peter Morgane also had obtained one of the respirators and had reported on the successful use of nitrous oxide, sometimes called "laughing gas," in anesthetizing dolphins.

Back at Point Mugu we tried to put the Lags to sleep with nitrous oxide. The equipment worked well. We were able to keep the dolphins on the respirator for an hour or more, but our tests of their reflexes, eyelid closure, and flipper movements showed that the dolphins were not sufficiently anesthetized for major surgery.

We did not want to keep testing the same dolphins because successive exposure to the anesthetic agents could damage their health. We also preferred bottle-nosed dolphins such as Tuffy because we would most likely treat these dolphins in the future. Five bottlenosed dolphins had been caught in Gulfport, Mississippi, so Wally, Marty, Ensign Harvey, and I flew there to experiment. Working night and day for a week at Gulfport, we anesthetized all these dolphins, thoroughly checking their reflexes to be sure they were insensitive to pain. We found that halothane, the anesthetic gas most commonly used in human surgery, also was effective for dolphins. We knew that we still had a great deal to learn about dolphin anesthesia—in fact, it would take two more years of careful work before Dr. James G. McCormick (then of Princeton University) and I finally perfected and documented the technique—but I felt confident that with the procedures we had developed at Gulfport, one of our dolphins with a threatening illness could be operated on in an emergency.

News of our medical success traveled rapidly in the small international community of dolphin keepers. I presented the findings at the American Veterinary

Medical Association's annual meeting in Portland, Oregon, in July 1965, and when I returned home at 10 P.M. from Portland, my wife greeted me with an urgent message: Hawaii was calling. Dr. Bill Evans, our dolphin sound expert, was spending the summer doing sonar research with the dolphins at Sea Life Park near Honolulu. Earlier that day the park's star performer, a bottlenosed dolphin named Keiki, had swallowed a net float. They had tried forcing the dolphin to upchuck the float, but it did not come up, and Keiki would not eat. All feared that he was failing rapidly. Would I come and operate? Tickets would be waiting at the Pan American counter at Los Angeles Airport.

I called Woody. "If they will pay your way, I see no reason why you shouldn't go," he said. "It would be good experience." I then called Ensign Harvey. He was sleepy but excited about the prospect of his first trip to Hawaii. After I explained that we would go directly to the lab, work through the remainder of the night to get our equipment ready, then go to Los Angeles to catch the first available flight, he was not as excited, but he still agreed to go.

Unshaven and slightly disheveled, we arrived at Los Angeles Airport with several large boxes of dolphin anesthesia equipment. I gave my name at the Pan Am desk and waited to hear whether our travel arrangements were in order. A smart-looking man in a blue blazer emerged from a doorway behind the counter, stepped across the luggage scales to us, and to my surprise said, "Yes, sir, follow me. The porter will bring your boxes."

"So you two are going to operate on the dolphin?" asked the stewardess as she seated us in the front cabin.

"How did you know that?" I asked.

"Oh, it's been on the news," she replied, then continued on a different subject. "May I get you guys a drink?"

"I'll have a double martini and a pillow," replied Frank. For an ensign, I thought, he was settling down rather quickly to the luxury of first class. As for me, I was a little numb after the meeting in Portland, the flight back, and working through the night to get here.

"I'll have the same, and an extra olive," I told the stewardess. Turning to Frank, I said, "Let's have a drink and something to eat, then we should get some sleep."

"Right," yawned Frank. "I could use some sleep."

There were no more than a half-dozen other passengers in the first-class cabin, with three stewardesses to serve our every need. Soon all nine people knew that Frank and I were going to Hawaii to operate on a dolphin. One woman told us that her late husband had been rescued by dolphins when he was shot down by the Japanese during World War II. She thought that to heal an animal like a dolphin surely must be the highest human calling. She toasted us. Frank and I, to be polite, toasted her.

An oil man wearing a big belt buckle, cowboy boots, and a Hawaiian shirt told us, "I used to fish those dolphins out of Havana. Good fish, lot of fight. 'Course the big game was marlin—damn that Castro, spoiled a lot of good fishing." Through another drink we explained to him the difference between the dolphin fish and the dolphin mammal.

Our need to sleep vanished in the warm glow of notoriety, fleeting sobriety, and the conviviality of this small, merry group at thirty-seven thousand feet. When the big jet nosed down for a landing in Honolulu, the arrival seemed somewhat anticlimactic. In the bright tropical sunshine and humid warmth of the Honolulu air, I soon began to feel drowsy. It was Frank who first realized we were drunk, just before two of the United States' leading dolphin researchers, Dr. Kenneth Norris and Dr. Bill Evans, met us at the baggage area. "Better think of some way to stall," said Frank. "You're in no condition to operate."

"I'll just reach in and pull it out," I grinned. Frank cringed and feigned a smile as he prepared to shake hands with Profesor Norris. Frank was greatly relieved to learn that no bottled oxygen was available at Sea Life Park. Before we could go and examine Keiki, a detour would have to be made for oxygen cylinders.

The sun was getting low in the west when I finally saw Keiki in a clear, blue pool at Sea Life Park. As I cast a bloodshot eye on the precious bottlenosed dolphin, Frank got out the respirator and managed to get it working. With a puff it would blow up a large balloon almost to the breaking point, hold it inflated for twenty seconds, then deflate the balloon and fill it again—just what Keiki would require when under anesthesia.

Sea Life's vet showed me x-rays taken earlier in the day. The float was definitely in the first stomach compartment. "I think we'll pull it out," I announced. From the expressions on the faces around me, I gathered that I'd better explain. "He's a small dolphin," I said. "Maybe I can put my hand through his mouth and reach into his stomach to pull the float out."

"But isn't your arm a little large for Keiki's throat?" asked a concerned Karen Pryor, Keiki's trainer.

"Perhaps we can find someone with a long, thin arm," I replied. "Maybe Tap can do it." Taylor A. Pryor, Karen's husband, ran Sea Life Park and was about six feet tall and slim, appearing to me more like a Wall Street broker or a Washington lawyer than a man who kept porpoises. Tap had a long, slender arm and a handshake that suggested he had sufficient strength to do the job.

Although he wouldn't eat, Keiki didn't look uncomfortable. "Let's wait the night," I suggested. "Tomorrow we can measure all the park staff and pick the person with the longest slender-yet-strong arm. I can practice him for a time, then we can have a go at Keiki by early afternoon at the latest." That seemed to satisfy everyone. Nobody seemed to notice how much the delay pleased Frank and me.

The next day the measurements showed that Tap Pryor had the arm most likely to reach Keiki's stomach. I had him practice pulling a similar float from a bucket full of mineral oil. I reasoned that this would get him ready to handle the slippery float inside Keiki. When Tap was ready, we placed Keiki on a canvas-covered operating stretcher. The dolphin was strapped down with automobile seat belts. Since this procedure could be done rapidly with the dolphin awake, I decided not to risk anesthesia.

A local cardiologist was there with his machine to watch the EKG. Frank was ready with the respirator if Keiki stopped breathing. Just outside our makeshift operating room where Keiki was strapped to his stretcher on a conference table, a small crowd gathered. Reporters were there with cameras and tape recorders. Under such scrutiny, I was glad to be clear-headed, or at least to feel so.

Keiki whistled repeatedly as I put a black rubber hood fashioned from a diver's wet suit over his head to protect his eyes if he thrashed his head from side to side during the procedure. I placed a rubber-padded speculum, normally used to hold a horse's mouth open for dentistry, in Keiki's mouth.

The whistles grew louder and seemed to take on a more urgent tone as I adjusted the speculum, making Keiki "say ahh" wider than he liked. I told Tap to put his hand down the dolphin's throat. As he pushed hard, Keiki gagged and bucked slightly against his restraint. Tap could not get his elbow past the jaws of the speculum.

We opened the speculum wider and lubricated Tap's arm. On the next entry Tap described the rougher feeling on his finger tips. That meant he had barely reached the forestomach where the float rested. It looked as if Tap's arm was about four inches too short.

"No cardiac activity," said the cardiologist. Tap pulled his hand out of Keiki's throat so Keiki could breathe. We watched anxiously. In a few seconds I was relieved to hear Keiki blow and the machine record the heartbeat's return.

I realized that we could give Tap another five or six inches by removing the speculum. Although this exposed Tap's arm to the dolphin's sharp teeth, he stuck his hand in and pushed as we held Keiki's mouth open with towels. Tap was right up to his armpit in the dolphin's throat, man and dolphin choking and straining.

"I've got my fingers on it," Tap said.

"No cardiac activity," the cardiologist said.

"I've got it! I'm coming out." But pull as hard as he

might, Tap could not seem to get his hand out through the dolphin's throat.

"Help him pull! You guys grab his waist," I ordered.

The largest trainer and two assistants stepped in and yanked Tap out of the dolphin. The offending plastic float fell plink, plink, plink across the concrete floor.

"The heart is beating," said the cardiologist.

Keiki snorted, and in three minutes he was back in his pool. A minute after that the dolphin was eagerly taking fish from Karen Pryor's hand. In a few days Keiki went back to work as a performer at Sea Life Park, apparently unharmed by the incident. The float that Keiki had swallowed had been used as a reward in tests that Karen was doing with the dolphin. Like Keller Breland's coin-stealing turkey and the baseball-playing dolphin back at Marineland, Keiki apparently had gotten the float confused with food. To avoid this problem, Karen switched to large wooden disks that were impossible to swallow.

Although Keiki was saved without anesthesia or surgery, other dolphins had conditions that were not so easily treated. By using the respirator and the anesthesia methods that we developed, I was able to perform surgery on dolphins that probably would have died if left untreated.

Sometime later, perhaps because I was dwelling more than I realized on the occasional successes of my research, I had a bizarre dream in which I figured in a gridiron contest between the Los Angeles Rams and the Pittsburgh Steelers. As usual, the Steelers played rough, but for this big game at the Los Angeles Coliseum they had concocted a particularly dirty strategy.

At the beginning of the fourth quarter, with the score tied, the Steelers had constructed a barbed wire barricade along their twenty-yard line. From there on past the goal posts the Steelers had created a water-covered marsh to prevent the Rams from getting to the goal line and scoring a touchdown. Ram coach George Allen suspected that the end zone marsh was inhabited by alligators that the Steelers had imported from Mississippi. The coach told me he could not afford to lose any of his players to alligators. "Dr. Ridgway," he said. "I want you to go in there and anesthetize those alligators!"

More than anxious to help, I pulled on a white doctor's coat over an ill-fitting football uniform, and with stethoscope and syringe protruding from my coat pocket, I scurried onto the Coliseum turf. In the huddle, Roman Gabriel, the Rams' quarterback, said, "Doc, my men aren't afraid of the Steelers, and we can get past the barbed wire, that's no problem. But nobody wants to risk being eaten by those alligators in the end zone. We think we can hold them until you can get down there and anesthetize those alligators. The tight end will jump on the barbed wire, and the split end will run right across his back and go over the goal line to receive my pass for a touchdown. You got it?"

I nodded affirmatively.

"OK," he said. "Let's have good blocking on two."

Somehow I was miraculously transported past the evil Steelers and arrived at the edge of the end zone marsh. I saw immediately that the Steelers had made a serious mistake in species identification. I yelled back to Gabriel. "These aren't alligators. They're dolphins!"

As the split end caught the perfectly thrown pass in

the end zone for the winning touchdown, I motioned to the dolphins to follow me. Obediently, five *Tursiops truncatus* rose out of the Coliseum marsh and trailed behind me, swimming through the air at a height of about six feet as I ran down the track surrounding the playing field and exited the stadium to the deafening roar of eighty thousand football fans. Obviously, my boyhood tendency toward Walter Mitty-type daydreams had not left my adult mind unaffected.

I had come in for some minor celebrity because of the dolphin rescue in Hawaii. Now Tuffy was due for some national attention of his own, as we were invited to join SeaLab II.

In September 1965, at the edge of Scripps Canyon just off La Jolla, California, the navy began the SeaLab II experiment. The objective was to test the ability of men to live and work at a depth of 205 feet, where the sea's pressure is more than six times that of the earth's atmosphere. A senior navy medical officer, Captain George Bond, was in charge of the experiment. Astronaut Scott Carpenter, who was to become the first man to live both in outer space and under the sea, was to lead the team of divers.

Diving to two hundred feet was risky for humans. Since air is poisonous at this pressure, the fifty-seven-foot-long, white metal canister that served as the bottom habitat for the SeaLab II divers would be filled with a special breathing mixture composed of 80 percent helium, 16 percent nitrogen, and 4 percent oxygen. Breathing this mixture, the SeaLab divers could acclimatize to the sea's pressure so they could spend hours each day working on the ocean bottom. After a short period on the ocean bottom, the aquanauts' body tissues would be saturated with gas under a pressure of more than one hundred pounds per square inch. If they popped to the surface, their bodies literally would explode. Therefore, when a SeaLab diver went outside the habitat, he had to plan his expedition carefully, making sure he could return to the habitat before exhausting the oxygen in the mixed gas supply carried on his back. Visibility was expected to be poor at this depth, and since humans have poor directional hearing underwater, the divers could not rely on sound to guide them back to the habitat. A lost aquanaut could be in real trouble.

The visibility problem was so serious that SeaLab divers would be tethered to the habitat so they could follow the line home or even be towed in if necessary. This would eliminate some of the risk for SeaLab II divers, but plans for future SeaLabs called for working at greater depths, with the aquanauts moving about freely. Captain Bond thought a dolphin might be trained to rescue a lost aquanaut, and he was eager to test this idea during SeaLab II. Since we had shown that Tuffy could easily dive to the SeaLab habitat at 205 feet, our dolphin was the most logical candidate for the tests.

The SeaLab II habitat was to be ready by September. We had just six weeks to prepare our equipment and our dolphin. The plan was to have each diver wear a sounding device. When a "lost" diver switched on the sounder, Tuffy would dive from the surface to the SeaLab habitat, pick up a rescue line from another diver, and swim out to the lost aquanaut, who would take the line from Tuffy and swim down it to the habitat. We also planned to have Tuffy deliver tools and messages from the surface to the divers and between groups of aquanauts working on the bottom.

Tuffy was perfectly adapted for the sea bottom pressure, but the strobe we used to call the dolphin was not. Our divers could hear the click of the strobe only a short distance and had relied on seeing the flashing of the strobe. At SeaLab the calling diver would be well out of sight on the cold, dark bottom. As a solution, engineers jury-rigged a loud, battery-powered doorbell buzzer inside a tube that the diver could wear on his arm and reach over to turn on when he wanted to call Tuffy.

On August 2, 1965, we started training Tuffy for SeaLab. Joining in our spirit of adventure, Woody gave our effort an official name: Project Arion. Having nothing like the SeaLab habitat at Point Mugu, we decided that Tuffy would have to learn about the habitat when we introduced him to it at the SeaLab location off La Jolla. We had the next best thing, however: Captain Bond loaned us aquanauts Ken Conda and John Reeves to help train Tuffy. They would be the primary divers for Tuffy's work at the SeaLab habitat.

Ken, a stocky, muscular diver with a quick smile, had no experience with dolphins, but John, a tall, easygoing photodiver, had been present on that Sunday morning in September 1962 when Tuffy, Dash, and the other dolphins were captured in Mississippi Sound; he had taken pictures of the capture and the subsequent transport of the dolphins to Point Mugu. As we started to train Tuffy for SeaLab, Ken and John assisted Marty and his crew on the ocean bottom, while Wally and I tried to keep things straight at the surface.

Tuffy had made dives with the heartbeat transmitter attached to his harness but never with tools, packages, mail pouches, or rescue lines. We were concerned that Tuffy might be shy of the trailing rescue line, and even more worried about the possibility that he might get the line tangled around his flukes or flippers and injure himself.

First we had to teach Tuffy to come to a diver sounding a buzzer and only to that diver. Tuffy was accustomed to zipping down and checking out any diver who happened to be on the bottom, whether he was called with the strobe or not. After a day in Tuffy's pen the divers learned to reward the dolphin only when he came to the buzzer when called. The dolphin had to keep his snout against the buzzer until the diver turned it off. This would keep the dolphin still for a moment, giving the diver a chance to unsnap the cargo from Tuffy's harness.

Over the next three weeks we trained Tuffy to do all the tasks required for SeaLab. In the morning the divers worked at 130 feet—as deep as they could since we were not equipped to use the helium mixture—and in the afternoon at 80 feet. Tuffy would go to the buzzer signal and allow the diver to attach or detach something; if another diver signaled, he would swim over to transfer lines, tools, or message packets.

These sessions erased any doubts the aquanauts had about working with our dolphin. The divers had heard the often-repeated stories about dolphins saving drowning humans by pushing them toward the surface. Such stories worried the aquanauts because, in their situation, to be pushed to the surface would mean instant death. The practice sessions reassured them that Tuffy would not try this.

Another story the divers had heard was that dolphins will protect people from sharks. This interested them. What would Tuffy do if a shark came around SeaLab? they wondered. The large scar on the dolphin's side was ample evidence of a past encounter. Had Tuffy killed the shark in that confrontation? Would Tuffy now be afraid of sharks? I didn't have the answers, but during this time I received a disturbing piece of news from Kenneth Norris, who had used a similar buzzer in diving experiments with a dolphin in Hawaii. During one of the experiments, the dolphin swam away from the researchers and never returned. The scientists theorized that the buzzer attracted sharks that frightened the dolphin, causing it to flee.

I asked Dr. Scott Johnson, an expert on both sharks and underwater sound, what he thought about the theory that the buzzer might attract sharks. "Yes," Scott said. "The low-frequency component of the buzzer sound possibly could attract sharks. It might resemble the thrashings of a wounded sea animal or some other such sound that would draw a shark." This news was unnerving, but it was too late to have different devices constructed and retrain Tuffy. Since no one was really certain that the buzzers attracted sharks, I decided not to trouble the divers with the speculation. I could do the worrying from the surface.

For the next week we practiced Tuffy twice a day on all his tasks. But the week after that, the dolphin quit working, as if he suddenly had forgotten what to do. He would dive to the buzzer, pick up a rescue line from the diver, then bring the line back to the surface to Wally rather than delivering it to the second diver on the bottom. Other times he would swim around the divers but never go to their buzzers. We began to panic. SeaLab was only a week away, and Tuffy wasn't ready.

I telephoned Debbie about the problem. "I don't think he likes to do the same thing over and over for a long time," she said. "Perhaps you should give him something else to do to break up the monotony."

I raised the question with Wally. "That could be right," said Wally. "You know, when I work elephants for the movies, the director always wants you to do a dry run just to see how it looks before he turns on the cameras. Then he'll want the elephant to do the trick again and again. I learned to refuse those dry runs and make them shoot the first one because the animal might not keep doing it all day."

We brought the divers back to the surface and started over from scratch with them in Tuffy's pen. Wally added some simple tricks that could relieve the monotony between dives. He would have the dolphin tail-walk or roll over to have his belly rubbed. In two days Tuffy was back doing all his tasks with the divers on the bottom.

Everything was ready. Mo had built another portable pen and trucked it down to La Jolla, where he assembled it on the beach, towed it out through the surf, and anchored it near SeaLab. Woody requested a helicopter to take Tuffy to San Diego. We retrieved Tuffy with the DUWK and drove the dolphin in the rear of a pickup to the taxiway where the orange helicopter was waiting. We put another foam pad in the helo, then groaned with the effort as we lifted Tuffy's 275-pound body through the narrow chopper door and onto the pad. Tuffy rested peacefully on the pad, his eye moving back and forth, up and down, following the human activity around him. It was hard to believe this was the same animal that, three years ago, had thrashed so violently each time we tried to handle him. Soon we were airborne, bound for San Diego.

Coming in over Mission Bay at San Diego, we landed near a dock at Quivira Basin. We carried Tuffy out and laid him on a lawn beside our landing spot. The gray dolphin, covered by a moist white sheet, appeared incongruous on the green grass. I sponged the dolphin while Marty and Wally checked out the boat that was to carry us to the SeaLab site. Since the dolphin blinked in the bright sunlight, I pulled the cotton sheet over his eye for shade.

Some reporters were clustered around asking questions. Cameramen snapped pictures as we lifted Tuffy and toted the dolphin over to the orange-and-gray boat that was to take us for an hour's ride to the holding pen in the ocean. When we arrived, Marty and I jumped down and fastened lines to Tuffy's temporary home. We stood on the narrow plank at one edge while navy men and reporters helped Wally lift Tuffy over the side and roll him into the water.

The dolphin swam a couple of quick laps around his pen, then came up open-mouthed, squealing and nodding in the direction of Wally on the boat above. I leaned back against the boat and looked across mild blue swells toward the sandy beaches and green hills of La Jolla rising out of the Pacific. On the hillsides the windows and walls of houses sparkled in the sun. Wally fed Tuffy and had the dolphin do a few tricks for the cameramen as we bobbed in the shadow of the boat.

When we began work the next morning, Tuffy appeared energetic. We planned to spend two days getting the dolphin accustomed to the area before we started the tests near the habitat. Early on that day Tuffy made seven dives. In the afternoon he made eight more. On each dive the dolphin required just a little over a minute to go down to the first diver, transfer a tool or package, swim over to the second diver carrying the rescue line, then swim back to the surface. Tuffy's performance amazed the divers, because he could do underwater work with such ease and return to the surface so quickly. The divers could remain on the bottom only a short time without going through decompression.

Captain Bond came over on the following day to dive with our crew. Working at 170 feet, Captain Bond was pleased with Tuffy's performance. "Tomorrow we can send him to the habitat," he said. At 9 A.M. Wally harnessed Tuffy under an overcast sky as the pen bounced in a moderate swell. Wally untied the string that held the gate and let the metal framework fall as he pitched a cube of mackerel in the Pacific just outside the pen. The harnessed dolphin sped through the open gate and nipped up the mackerel cutlet before any ocean fish had a chance at it, then caught up with us to swim beside our small workboat. We tied the boat to a barge about 100 feet from the *Berkone,* the SeaLab "mothership" that floated directly over the habitat.

We waited. The dolphin lay at the surface, scanning the sea under him. What does he think about all this, I wondered. His sonar must be giving him a strange picture of the sea bottom. Tuffy probably could "image" the long canister of the habitat itself, the transport capsule that was used to bring divers still under pressure back to the surface for decompression, the many cables and hoses that ran from the *Berkone* to the habitat, the powerful lights that illuminated the habitat for the divers, and the myriad bubbles drifting up from divers and apparatus on the bottom.

When I listened on the hydrophone, I could barely hear the noises the dolphin made over the din of sound from the barges, machinery, and activity under the surface. Finally, though, I heard the buzzer. The divers were calling Tuffy. The dolphin dived, and I started the stopwatch. Tuffy usually took no more than twenty or thirty seconds to reach the diver, but for some reason there seemed to be a problem. The buzzer continued to sound, and after seventy seconds Tuffy appeared beside us again. He had not gone to the aquanauts.

Although they called him three more times, Tuffy refused to go to the men on the bottom. On the last two calls he made mock dives, going just under the surface and waiting a few seconds before coming right back to our boat. Captain Bond came out on the *Berkone*'s deck with his bullhorn and announced to the assemblage: "Tuffy did not go down." I felt sorry for Woody, who was on the *Berkone* and had to explain to the reporters why Tuffy had not performed as promised.

Tuffy followed close by our boat as we drove back to the diver-support craft. Wally gave the animal a rubdown, then had him do a few of his tricks and make a jump or two for the cameras. "The porpoise wants to work," said Wally. "He must be afraid of something over there."

We talked with Woody over the telephone in the

diver-support craft. Woody asked Captain Bond to have the aquanauts move a little farther out from the habitat and try again. I heard the buzzer go on, and Tuffy responded immediately. We waited. One hundred five seconds passed, but the dolphin returned to us without doing his job. After a short interval the buzzer sounded. Tuffy dived. I started the stopwatch. A full minute elapsed; the buzzer still sounded. Another minute passed, Tuffy did not return, and the divers still buzzed. Could sharks be coming to the buzzing? Could the dolphin's harness have gotten tangled on some of the apparatus below? Maybe Tuffy had simply left all the commotion and possible dangers behind and taken off into the open sea. I looked back toward the pen; Marty and Wally scanned the ocean around us. Finally, after four minutes and thirty seconds, we saw Tuffy's dorsal fin about one hundred feet from us. Wally put in the strobe. "Let's go back to the pen," he said when Tuffy poked the clicker.

Later we learned that on the last dive Tuffy had come within twenty feet of Ken and close enough to John to be touched but would not hold still for the line transfer. This tiny piece of good news encouraged us. We made a plan for the following day: The aquanauts would come out into an open area about one hundred feet from SeaLab. If Tuffy responded properly, they would move closer to the habitat.

The new plan worked. Tuffy responded promptly the next morning and went right to the buzzing diver. During the entire day Tuffy performed all his tasks without a hitch. The day after that the dolphin's performance again was flawless. He transferred the rescue lines with ease and speed. He could shoot to the bottom, do his job, and be back on the surface in just over a minute. Tuffy delivered tools, mail packets, and soft drinks; he even carried down plastic bags filled with the fish the aquanauts used to reward him for his good work.

The tests of Project Arion were finished, and the following official conclusion was drawn: "A dolphin can be trained to perform useful and even vital tasks in man-in-the-sea programs such as SeaLab. Once trained, the animal will perform with a high degree of precision and reliability and can adapt relatively quickly to a strange and, in many ways, disturbing environment. All of the ways in which a trained marine mammal can contribute have not been determined; it is expected that further investigations will be conducted."

These dry words don't fully convey the navy's excitement over Tuffy's pioneering success. Many officers were as thrilled as I was by Tuffy's cooperation and skill, and ambitious plans were laid for future dolphin work. To this day the navy continues to use dozens of dolphins in undersea programs. But Tuffy was the first.

On the last day of our SeaLab work we called Tuffy back to the sling so we could begin the trip back to Point Mugu. As we looked across the waves, I wondered what motivated the dolphin to return. He could have swum free in the open sea on his own. Schools of fish around us near the surface and around the divers on the bottom were ample evidence that he would not go hungry. Perhaps, for some reason, the dolphin felt more secure with us. Maybe we were now his "herd."

Not long after we returned from SeaLab, I resumed working on my plans to measure the maximum depth that Tuffy could dive. I told my plans to Wally. "We can put a buoy five miles at sea in deep water. Tuffy can swim out there in less than an hour, and we will have most of the day for diving."

Wally nodded and smiled, but for some reason he did not seem to listen carefully as I told him of my plans. A few minutes later he told me why. "You'll have to find someone else to work with Tuffy," he said. "Hollywood's going to shoot a big movie called Doctor Doolittle. I've signed on to train the elephants and sea lions."

Wally stayed at Point Mugu long enough to instruct his replacement, a likable young man named Blair Irvine whom I had met in Hawaii during the episode with Keiki. Blair actually had a longer arm than Tap Pryor, but his was more muscular and larger in diameter. If Tap had faltered, Blair had been ready to go in. Remembering this, I felt that Blair had the right temperament to work with Tuffy.

During Blair's indoctrination period we pumped Wally for hints about working with Tuffy. "The smartest animals I have worked with are elephants, chimps, and dolphins, but sea lions are easier to train," Wally told us. "I believe Tuffy is the smartest individual I have ever worked with. He keeps you thinking all the time. It's okay when you have him in a pen or in the tank, but when he's in the open ocean, you are at his mercy. You are strictly dependent on his cooperation. The funny thing is that he usually does cooperate when the chips are down. He could just leave us if he really wanted to."

Wally paused for a moment and looked across the surf toward Tuffy's pen. "Well, Doc," he drawled, "I'm going back to training elephants and sea lions. For a while, *I'm* going to be the teacher."

In many ways the year 1965 marked the pinnacle of Tuffy's accomplishments. We would continue to learn a great deal from him, but never again would the knowledge come so fast or the advances be so astonishing. Tuffy easily accomplished tasks that no human diver even could have tried. During the year after we first released him in Mugu Lagoon, working with him for hundreds of hours, we had learned how Tuffy functioned in shallow and deep water. Using telemetry, we had studied the responses of his heart and breathing as he dived and swam. We marveled at Tuffy's use of waves, his sonar, and his sensitive directional hearing.

Tuffy was still a young dolphin; we estimated his age at about six or seven years, and dolphins are thought to live to be twenty-five or older. I expected to be working with Tuffy for many years to come and never would have guessed that in less than five years our friendship would come to an end.

The years that followed the SeaLab II project were divided between navy projects and my own continuing research. Only a month after Tuffy's well-publicized exploits with SeaLab II, the navy asked whether the dolphin might assist in the recovery of a missile cradle. This cradle, a reusable framework for the Regulus missile, had fallen into the sea as the rocket went on its way. Before the shot the missile engineers had attached to the cradle one of the buzzers the SeaLab aquanauts had worn. We trained Tuffy to home in on the buzzer and guide divers to the cradle so they could retrieve the reusable hardware. Although the Regulus project was in its final days, the navy was interested in saving other test objects that had to be fired, dropped, or planted in the ocean. With Tuffy's help these recoveries soon became much easier.

There were many changes at Point Mugu at this time. Frank Harvey, promoted to lieutenant, departed for a new assignment, and a new ensign, Steve O'Brien, took charge of the ever-changing group of sailors that helped us keep our growing herd of dolphins. Mo built more pens for holding our trained dolphins in the ocean. A female named Pegasus joined Tuffy in his pen. (Pegasus was not a stranger to Tuffy. When Bob Bailey left for a permanent job at ABE in Arkansas, Marty took over the training of the dolphin Buzz Buzz, with whom Tuffy had shared a pool, and gave her a new name, Pegasus.) Meanwhile, scientists from universities nationwide continued to visit our facility to observe and study our dolphins.

To continue my diving experiments we received permission to use a large buoy in eighteen hundred feet of water, about six miles off Point Mugu. For this diving work we decided to leave off the harness, since Tuffy had backed out of the straps one day while working with divers on the bottom. Clearly he felt impeded; water drag on the straps slowed his swimming speed. We simply stopped using this last vestige of our physical power over the dolphin. Some less-tangible bonds held Tuffy.

Plans were being made for SeaLab III, where the diver habitat would be on the bottom at six hundred feet. We were sure that Tuffy could dive this deep, but to prove it we had to get more cable and build a new diving test device. The new switch contained a sounder, temperature sensor, and depth gauge in a plastic tube thirty inches long at the end of a thousand feet of cable. A plunger on the end of the tube switched off the sound when the dolphin pressed it.

In late spring we flew Tuffy to Panama City, Florida, for six weeks of practice with a SeaLab model installed on the ocean bottom in just sixty feet of water. I was sure the practice sessions would be useful, but I was concerned about the locale. Tuffy had been captured only five years before off Gulfport, Mississippi, less than two days of dolphin travel from the waters in the SeaLab practice area. Tuffy never had shown an inclination to join the Lags we sometimes saw near Point Mugu, but free in the warm Gulf waters, he might meet his old herd, his progenitors. I wondered what would happen then.

In the practice sessions in Florida, Tuffy learned to swim directly to the habitat on signal, take a loop of cloth from a rescue reel, and, as the reel unwound, pull a line out to a "lost" diver. The reel was spring-loaded so it would rewind, gently pulling the diver back to the habitat while Tuffy returned to the surface. Tuffy worked with strange divers and new equipment and practiced tool deliveries.

The results of the training sessions were satisfying, but Tuffy's reactions to herds of wild bottlenosed dolphins in the area were more interesting. Twice Blair Irvine encountered herds of these dolphins while running out to the practice site with Tuffy surfing on his wake. On one occasion, when Blair came upon a herd of about fifteen bottlenoses, Tuffy stayed on the wake close to Blair's boat, never once venturing out. He even bypassed some of the fish that Blair threw. Blair's impression was that Tuffy was wary of this dolphin group.

On the second occasion Blair encountered a larger herd, perhaps as many as forty animals. This time Tuffy left the boat and bolted toward the herd. But at Tuffy's approach the wild herd stampeded. Dolphins started, snorted, slapped their tails against the water, and swam away from Tuffy at full speed, making long leaps out of the water as they fled. In a few minutes Tuffy returned to surf on the stern wave of Blair's boat.

I was very glad when Tuffy arrived back at Point Mugu. Those who said we could not work with a dolphin free in the open sea—where it has access to abundant food, is free to join herds of its own species, and is free to roam the ocean—obviously were wrong. Those who expressed moral outrage at our capture and training of dolphins for our research certainly must now reconsider. Those individuals, whose identity we probably will never know, who once opened the gate of Tuffy's and Pegasus's pen and lured them to "freedom," must now have second thoughts. (It took two days to locate Tuffy, who was found playing in a kelp bed about twenty miles up the coast. He willingly returned when Blair called him. The next day Pegasus appeared near a fishing boat, following it a few miles back to her pen.)

At Point Mugu we continued Tuffy's deep-diving tests and other preparations for SeaLab III. But the SeaLab III schedule kept slipping, and after a fatal accident in the project we received word that it had been canceled. Nevertheless, the diving studies with Tuffy had been instructive. Diving to six hundred feet is a dangerous undertaking for humans, but as our work with Tuffy showed, descent to these depths could be a natural act of daily life for a dolphin. We were not sure why this was so. What secrets of dolphin physiology allowed these mammals to race back and forth from surface to depth with such ease? To find out, we wanted to determine how quickly Tuffy depleted his oxygen store during a dive. We needed to analyze samples of Tuffy's exhaled air after deep dives, so I called Dr. Kanwisher at Woods Hole Oceanographic Institution to follow up on our old deal. He was eager to come to California to help us analyze Tuffy's breath.

At first, as we prepared for the breath analysis, we wasted a lot of time trying to get the dolphin to stick his head out of the water, seal his blowhole against a valve, and exhale through the valve into a collecting bag. Because we could not seal the valve quickly enough, we always got an unknown amount of outside air with the sample. Tuffy helped us solve the problem. One day as I watched him poised three or four feet underwater, he exhaled a large bubble that boiled near me on the surface. This underwater bubble-blowing was something all our dolphins did from time to time, apparently to get our attention. Suddenly I realized that I had the answer. We could put a large funnel under the water and Tuffy could be trained to blow his bubble directly into it.

Once we got the idea, it took us only fifteen minutes to teach Tuffy to exhale into the funnel. An underwater buzzer was Tuffy's signal to perform. If he pushed his snout against the buzzer and exhaled into the underwater funnel just above it, he received three smelts as a reward. Another buzzer served as a signal for Tuffy to submerge and hold his snout on a station just below the surface. By varying the interval between the submerge buzzer and the collection buzzer, we obtained samples of exhaled air over Tuffy's entire range of breath-holding times. Tuffy could hold his breath easily for as long as six minutes, but after a much shorter time he grew impatient as he waited for the collection buzzer to sound; looking up through the water at us, he even would gnash his teeth.

Studying the data Tuffy provided us, John Kanwisher and I were astounded at how quickly the oxygen concentration in the dolphin's lungs dropped off. For example, after only three minutes the gas in Tuffy's lungs had fallen from its normal level of 21 percent oxygen to less than 2 percent. For the remaining three minutes of these "easy" dives, he was virtually running without oxygen. After such a breath-hold, he would not submerge again until he had spent four or five minutes breathing rapidly on the surface, repaying the oxygen debt he had incurred. After dives of two or three minutes, however, he would readily dive again, following only a brief breathing interval at the surface.

We now could understand why we had not observed an abruptly diminished heart rate when Tuffy dived.

Clearly, he made only a partial effort, if any at all, to conserve his initial store of oxygen. That store was consumed quickly; thereafter, an oxygen debt developed in the tissues, including the brain. Usually the dolphin tried to avoid such an oxygen debt by limiting his dives to short periods. When Tuffy and our other dolphins swam without instructions to the contrary, dives lasting more than two and one-half minutes were the exception rather than the rule. Submerging for shorter intervals, the dolphins might continue diving for hours to depths of six hundred to eight hundred feet.

With other questions in mind we continued to urge Tuffy to dive deeper and deeper. We knew that this did not endanger him, since he would refuse to go any deeper than was physically possible. Finally Tuffy was diving to the end of our one thousand feet of cable. After these deeper dives Tuffy needed some time to recover. The dolphin stayed at the surface, breathing more rapidly for several minutes, before he would dive again. He obviously was approaching his limit.

Yet Tuffy seemed unaffected by the increasing water pressure at greater depths. We expected that at such a high external pressure the animal's lungs would be almost completely collapsed. By rigging the dive plunger with a flash camera, we were able to photograph Tuffy as he turned off the buzzer a thousand feet below us. The photographs showed that indeed his rib cage was greatly deformed by the hydrostatic pressure on his lungs. Far from being a handicap, this deformation helped prevent the bends. The pressure collapsed the tiny air cavities in the lung (the alveoli) and prevented nitrogen in the lung air from going into circulation, thus preventing the bends after these deep dives.

In 1969 we published the results of our studies in the journal *Science,* acknowledging Tuffy's contribution as follows: "This work was made possible through the outstanding cooperation and performance of a singularly unique *Tursiops truncatus* that we named 'Tuffy' because of his humanlike frailty of occasionally displaying an ill temper." The sense of this statement was, for me, absolutely sincere. In all the work I did with Tuffy, I always believed that this dolphin's contributions were special, that his intelligent cooperation made it possible for us to learn more from him.

A year later, in the spring of 1970, I knelt beside the pool watching Tuffy as he slept. With closed eyes he drifted in the mild current created by pumps that moved seawater from Mugu Pier through the pool. Over the past eight years I had spent many hours in contemplation watching Tuffy. I had come to respect his intelligence, but I knew that it must be of a different order than that of humans. Despite its size and impressive similarities, the dolphin brain, I knew, was different from ours. Perhaps it is impossible for us to conceive how such a brain might perceive the world. Tuffy's gray matter was cut from a different cloth. Nevertheless, when I watched him free in the ocean or at play in his sea pen, when he pouted or angrily bit his trainer or squealed in apparent glee, when he stared at me with a dark, alert eye, I thought I glimpsed some shared pattern in that cloth.

Tonight, as I watched Tuffy drift around his pool, I was heartsick: I knew that Tuffy probably was near death. A bacterial infection never before encountered in a dolphin had stiffened his lower body, almost paralyzing the powerful tail muscles that once had swept him through the sea. *(Clostridial myositis* was our name for the disease, an ailment commonly called blackleg in cattle.)

We do not know how Tuffy contracted the infection. Ten days earlier we had seen an oozing wound on Tuffy's underside. As soon as possible we brought Tuffy from his sea pen back to the pool for treatment. On the underside of Tuffy's flank near the genital slit, one of a pair of pores—openings of a gland we still do not understand—was inflamed and swollen. Hoping that it was treatable and not life-threatening, I cleaned the lesion and began antibiotic treatment. At first Tuffy seemed to improve, but soon the signs of muscular stiffness became increasingly apparent. Although we tried everything available to us, no treatment was effective.

After a short illness, Tuffy died. All of us who had worked with him grieved for the loss of his marvelously complex life. For me it was not so much that I had lost a valuable research animal, although that was true. Far more important was that I had lost a beloved friend who had helped me to learn more about my world and his. I was consoled by the knowledge that Tuffy's unique personality and exploits would live on in the memories of those who worked with him and in the annals of science. I was especially moved because my involvement with Tuffy had launched my own absorbing lifework. Tuffy was with us for only eight years, but what a time it was!

Afterword

At death Tuffy weighed three hundred pounds, and according to Dr. Clifford Hui's analysis of his teeth, he was twelve years old. I believe he was entering the "growth spurt" period that I have seen male dolphins go through before reaching full sexual maturity. This might be an especially stressful time for male dolphins.

The cycle of dolphins' lives under the sea remains largely a mystery. For example, we still cannot improve on Aristotle's estimate that dolphins live about 25 years. Numerous dolphin births in captivity, however, have helped us piece together parts of the puzzle. The dolphin mother carries her calf for 12 months, producing a calf about 3 1/2 feet long and weighing 35 or 40 pounds. Within seconds of birth the calf can swim and call with a shrill whistle. The mother nurses her calf on rich milk for 18 months or longer, although in the latter two-thirds of this nursing period the dolphin calf begins to take small fish as part of its daily food. By weaning age, the dolphin might weigh 150 pounds or more, and its brain will have grown to about 80 percent of its adult size. Female dolphins have conceived as early as six years of age, but most females probably are a few years older when they conceive and bear young. Although male calves only a week old have been seen with erections, bottlenosed dolphin males do not appear to become sexually mature until they are between ten and fifteen years of age.

Dr. John Simpson, a veterinary pathologist, performed a thorough postmortem examination on Tuffy. Bill Gilmartin, the microbiologist in our laboratory, identified the anaerobic bacteria that killed him from specimens of Tuffy's muscle and took some kidney stones for analysis. Even in death Tuffy furnished new scientific information.

After Tuffy's autopsy we stitched up the dolphin's body and took it to a taxidermist near San Diego, who made a precise fiberglass reproduction of Tuffy's remains. When this was finished, we cleaned the skull and kept it for future study. We returned the rest of Tuffy's body to the sea near our dive buoy off Point Mugu.

Not long afterward the Point Mugu facility closed. Some of the work started there continued in San Diego and Hawaii. About this time I received a fellowship to the University of Cambridge, England, to study under the supervision of Professor Richard J. Harrison. There I earned a Ph.D. in neurobiology. After that I came to San Diego, where I continue dolphin science and veterinary work with marine mammals. I live with my wife, Jeanette, on the edge of San Diego Bay.

The talented Debbie Duffield earned an M.S. at Stanford and a Ph.D. at UCLA. She now teaches college biology and does marine mammal research in Portland, Oregon. Marty Conboy and Bill Scronce still work for the navy—Marty in Hawaii and Bill in San Diego. Mo Wintermantel, who retired in 1984, still works with me occasionally. Wally Ross lives in Thousand Oaks, California, where he trains animals for the movie industry.

Although Keller Breland is deceased, ABE of Hot Springs, Arkansas, is still the leader in the animal behavior business. Bob Bailey, the first head dolphin trainer at Point Mugu, now works at ABE. F.G. Wood, our facility director at Point Mugu, has retired in San Diego but continues to be active in marine mammal science.

Although some of my good friends and leaders in dolphin science are psychologists, I don't hear from any of those whom I characterized under the fictional name of Dr. Veruccus. I assume "he" is teaching psychology somewhere in the Midwest. Veruccus's main experimental dolphin, Dash, a fully mature male weighing more than 450 pounds, is still in my care.

I am still fascinated by dolphins. I want to know about their large brains. I want to know how they make their sounds and what those sounds mean. I want to know how to keep them healthy in captivity and protected from human enterprise in the wild. Although I see other dolphins every day and never tire of their friendly exuberance, I still remember Tuffy as a special individual. I have since seen bottlenosed dolphins that could dive deeper and swim faster than Tuffy. But I have not seen a dolphin that showed me as much cleverness and apparent understanding of its human companions.

I remember one day, one of many similar days,

when the sun shone from a bright blue sky on a crystal-clear Pacific. We spent that day at the dive buoy watching Tuffy dive into the smoky blue abyss. Then we waited expectantly for his dark eyes to appear out of the depths as he watched us watching him. I can see him riding large waves, I can see the crescent scar as he leaped above the surf chasing a school of anchovies, and I can hear his squeal of glee. As we motored in, Tuffy riding the stern wave of our boat, I remember thinking, For me, life can't get any better than this, and if I could translate his thoughts into human terms, I bet Tuffy might be thinking the same thing.

About the Author

Born in the rangeland of South Texas, Dr. Sam Ridgway moved to California in 1960 and fell in love with the sea and its creatures. Ridgway has worked with dolphins for all but two years of his medical career; in 1974 he received a Ph.D. in neurobiology from the University of Cambridge. As a ground-breaking veterinarian, he has traveled worldwide to lecture on the care and physiology of marine mammals. He lives in San Diego with his wife, Jeanette.

Finally Fawcett has the purrr-fect Pet Care Books